D1100528

PIMP YOUR AIR FRYER

If you are hoping for a standard air fryer cookbook, walk away now!

PIMP YOUR AIR FRYER

JAKE GRIGG

SIMON &
SCHUSTER

London · New York · Sydney · Toronto · New Delhi

PIMP YOUR AIR FRYER
First published in Australia in 2022 by
Simon & Schuster (Australia) Pty Limited
Suite 19A, Level 1, Building C, 450 Miller Street, Cammeray, NSW 2062

10 9 8 7 6 5 4 3 2 1

Sydney New York London Toronto New Delhi
Visit our website at www.simonandschuster.com.au

© Jake Grigg 2022

All rights reserved. No part of this publication may be reproduced, stored in a
retrieval system, or transmitted in any form or by any means, electronic, mechanical,
photocopying, recording or otherwise, without prior permission of the publisher.

 A catalogue record for this
book is available from the
National Library of Australia

ISBN: 9781761104695

Cover and internal design: Meng Koach
Cover photography: Lawrence Furzey Photography
Cover and internal illustrations: Brent Smith
Printed and bound in Australia by Griffin Press

FSC
MIX
Paper
FSC® C009448

The paper this book is printed on is certified
against the Forest Stewardship Council®
Standards. Griffin Press holds chain of custody
certification SGSHK–COC–005088. FSC®
promotes environmentally responsible, socially
beneficial and economically viable management
of the world's forests.

for my nephew, Nate.

CONTENTS

INTRODUCTION

If you are hoping this is a standard air fryer cookbook, please close the pages, put the book back on the shelf and walk away. This book is not for you.

I'm tired of the same old cookbooks with the same old recipes, so I decided to make something that goes against the grain: a recipe book that is not only super fun and light-hearted, but one that promotes creativity and challenges the fundamentals of cooking.

My name is Jake and until recently, I was just a regular human man who enjoyed cooking. Then I started making air fryer cooking videos on TikTok and Instagram under the name @airfryerguy. Nowadays, I'm still a human man, but one with an audience. That's a scary thought!

I don't have a cooking background and I'm definitely not a qualified chef, but I love cooking and I'm creative. My background is in music, which is why I partner all my TikTok recipes with jingles. 'You gotta put it in the air fryyyyya.' I believe that cooking should be fun and creative and that is exactly the vibe of this book.

My parents are great cooks and I have fond memories of watching them dancing, singing and hugging in the kitchen while cooking together. Dinner was a family event – we always ate together at the table and talked about our day. Most nights we would ask each other about our favourite foods and why we liked or disliked certain foods. Mum loved creating new recipes and, without fail, they always tasted great. Dad used to take me to the bakery after school and we dreamed about owning our own bakery one day, joking that it wasn't possible because we would eat all of the stock. I've always had a huge appetite.

Air fryers are a phenomenon. I don't think there has been this much hype about a kitchen appliance since the microwave. I've tried putting everything and anything into an air fryer – from fairy floss to watermelon, you name it, I've air fried it! But one thing is for sure, air frying is amazing and it's here to stay. Whether you have just bought

an air fryer and you are still learning the tricks of the trade, or you are an air fryer OG and looking to take your air frying to the next level, you will already know how incredible that little machine is. It's changed my life and the lives of many people around the world. Who would've thought that hot circulating air could have so much power?

I hope you enjoy these recipes and they inspire you to get creative in the kitchen. Just remember: it's all about having fun.

A BIT ABOUT AIR FRYERS

New to air frying? Well, sorry to disappoint you but air fryers aren't really fryers. They are full of hot air and use air rather than fat for cooking. So your fish and chips might taste a little different from your favourite takeaway shop when cooked in an air fryer BUT they will be much less messy, use way less fat, be crispy and taste just as good, if not better!

My five tips for using an air fryer:

1. Don't overcrowd. Leave plenty of space so air can circulate around the food. That is what gives you crispy results.
2. Before you begin, always spray the basket with cooking oil so nothing sticks unless the recipe uses baking paper.
3. Don't be scared to open the air fryer as often as you like to check on your food. You won't lose much heat, it's not an oven!
4. Use toothpicks to hold down light food. It gets windy in there!
5. Air fryers cook food quickly, so if you are cooking something that has packet instructions for an oven, you can almost half the cooking time.

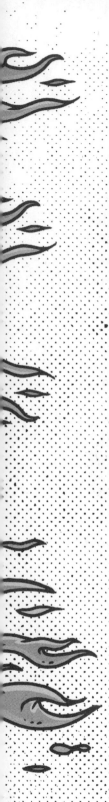

RECIPES AND RHYMES

I **used to suck at remembering recipes. I just couldn't**
remember every step because my brain chose to focus on other
important issues, such as would people still like me if I had two
noses? Who nose?

Anyway, I did learn a way to trick my brain into remembering
recipes without having to focus too much. How? Jingles and rhymes.
For every recipe I made, I would make up a little rhyme using the steps
and ingredients as the lyrics and sing a tune while I was cooking. So,
the next time I cooked that recipe, I just had to remember the song
rather than the method.

Alongside each of these recipes will be a rhyme to help you
remember the steps ...

♪ *You gotta put it in the air fryer* ♪♪

EASY PEASY PIZZA TOAST

This is the easiest snack and really quick to cook,
With only four ingredients, you need to have a look.
Place the bread onto a plate then get your pizza sauce,
Spread the sauce onto the bread using a knife, of course.
Add pepperoni and cheese, then press it down a bit,
So the cheese will stay in place when you air fry it.
Then put it in the air fryer at 180 degrees,
Celsius, of course – for six minutes, please.

Makes 2
2 slices bread
2 tablespoons pizza sauce
6 slices pepperoni
2 slices cheese

- Preheat air fryer to 180°C.
- Place slices of bread onto a plate or flat surface and spread pizza sauce evenly over the bread, making sure to completely cover the bread.
- Place slices of pepperoni on top of the sauce and a slice of cheese on top of the pepperoni. Slightly press the cheese down into the bread so that it sticks to the sauce and doesn't go flying around the air fryer. *(If you find that the cheese won't stay in place during cooking, secure it with a toothpick.)*
- Place the pizzas into the air fryer and cook at 180°C for 6 minutes, or until the cheese is melted and golden and the bread is toasty.

FERRERO ROCHER POPPERS

Get your puff pastry, cut out some rounds,
If you don't have a cutter use a bowl upside down.
Put a Ferrero in the middle of the disc,
Then fold the pastry over and press it down a bit.
Use a fork to seal the edges so nothing can escape,
Then cover it with butter – this will make the pastry flake.
Cook it in the air fryer until it's golden brown,
This delicious treat will turn your frown upside down!

Makes 8
2 sheets puff pastry, thawed
8 Ferrero Rochers
2 tablespoons butter, melted

- Place puff pastry sheets onto a dry surface. Cut out eight 10 cm rounds. *(If you don't have a 10 cm circle cutter, you can use a small bowl. Place the bowl upside down on the pastry and trace around it with a sharp knife.)*
- Place a Ferrero Rocher into the centre of each pastry round. Fold the pastry round in half, encasing the Ferrero Rocher. Press down firmly around the edges of the pastry to seal. Use the pointy end of a fork to press around the edges to seal further, making a cute little indent pattern. Repeat with remaining pastry and Ferrero Rochers.
- Preheat air fryer to 180°C.
- Brush melted butter over all sides *(including the bottom)* of the pastries.
- In batches, place the pastries in the air fryer and cook at 180°C for 8–10 minutes or until the pastry is golden and flaky.
- Let the poppers cool slightly, then serve.

NUTELLA AND STRAWBERRY POP-TARTS

Dice up the berries and cut up the pastry,
Spread the Nutella, top with berries so tasty.
Put pastry on top then seal the sides,
Brush them with butter – we're getting there, guys!
Poke a few holes in the top of the tarts,
And now you are ready for the air frying part.
Cook for ten minutes until golden brown,
Drizzle with Nutella then eat it right now.

Makes 2

1 sheet shortcrust pastry, thawed
4 strawberries
3 tablespoons Nutella
1 tablespoon butter, melted

- Place pastry sheet onto a dry work surface. Cut into quarters and separate.
- On a chopping board, hull and dice strawberries.
- On the first two pieces of pastry, spoon and spread 1 tablespoon of Nutella on each, making sure to leave a 1 cm space around the edges of the pastry. (*Set aside the other tablespoon of Nutella for later.*) Then top with chopped strawberries.

- Brush some melted butter around the edges of the Nutella-topped pastries.
- Place the remaining two pieces of pastry on top. Using your finger, gently press down the edges of the pastry to seal. Then use a fork to crimp the edges and poke a few holes in the top (*for aesthetics and to let steam escape*). Cut off any excess pastry and brush the top with remaining butter.
- Preheat air fryer to 180°C.
- Place a piece of baking paper into the air fryer basket then put the tarts in and cook at 180°C for 10 minutes or until golden and crisp.
- Drizzle with remaining Nutella and serve.

AIR FRIED CHEESE AND BACON SANDWICH

Air fry the bacon, butter the bread,
Now build the sandwich – if you want to be fed.
Bread, cheese, bacon, cheese, bacon, cheese, bread,
It's as easy as that, now let's move ahead.
Into the air fryer to melt all the cheese,
And toast up the bread – so delicious indeed.
And when it's all golden with cheese oozing out,
Cut it in half then put it into your mouth.

Makes 1

2 rashers streaky bacon
2 slices bread
2 tablespoons butter
1 slice Swiss cheese
1 slice mozzarella cheese
1 slice tasty cheese

- Preheat air fryer to 180°C.
- Place bacon into the air fryer and cook at 180°C for 5–10 minutes, or until it reaches your desired crispiness. *(I prefer my bacon to cook for 7 minutes.)*
- Meanwhile, place a sheet of baking paper on a dry surface. Place the bread onto the paper and generously butter both sides of both pieces.
- Remove bacon from air fryer.

- Build the sandwich. Bread, Swiss cheese, bacon, mozzarella cheese, bacon, tasty cheese and finally the second piece of bread. Compress the sandwich slightly by applying downward pressure. *(This should keep the sandwich together while air frying, but if you find that your sandwich decides to fly around the air fryer, you can secure it with a toothpick.)*
- Place the sandwich into the air fryer *(no need to clean it after cooking the bacon)* and cook at 180°C for 7 minutes or until the bread is golden and toasty and the cheese is oozing.
- Cut sandwich in half and serve.

♫ *Today I'm going to make something nice in the aiiirr fryyyyyerrr* ♪

NATE'S SPAGHETTI POCKETS

Cut the crust off the bread and make a small indent,
Spoon in spaghetti, get it right in there.
Top with some cheese tasty, Swiss or parmesan,
Put the bread on top and press the edges to fasten.
Brush with melted butter all over the pockets,
Cook them in the air fryer – when the time is right, stop it.
Put them on a plate and get ready to eat,
These cute little easy delightful treats.

Makes 2
4 slices bread
220 g can spaghetti
¼ cup grated cheese
2 tablespoons butter, melted

- Preheat air fryer to 180°C.
- Cut the crusts off the bread. Make a small indent in the middle of two of the slices by pressing down with your fingers. (*This will help the spaghetti stay in place.*)
- Spoon spaghetti into the indents in the bread and top with grated cheese.
- Place the remaining bread on top of the spaghetti-filled slices and firmly press around the edges to seal.
- Brush melted butter over both sides of the bread pockets.
- Place pockets into the air fryer and cook at 180°C for 7 minutes or until the bread is golden and toasty.

SALT AND PEPPER PRAWNS

Peel the prawns then place into a bowl,
Add herbs and spices, then toss and roll.
Drizzle with oil and then toss them again,
Don't be afraid to get messy hands!
Place the prawns evenly inside the air fryer,
Cook for five minutes and turn as required.
Let the prawns rest for a slight bit of time,
Then serve with some sauce or drizzle with lime.

Serves 2–3
10 green king prawns, shell on
¼ teaspoon pepper
¼ teaspoon salt
1 teaspoon garlic powder
¼ teaspoon sugar
1½ teaspoons corn flour
1 tablespoon olive oil

- Peel and devein the prawns, leaving the tail on.
- Preheat air fryer to 200°C.
- Add pepper, salt, garlic, sugar and corn flour to a medium-sized bowl. Add the prawns to the bowl and toss well to coat in seasoning. Once coated, drizzle oil over prawns and toss again.
- Place the prawns in the air fryer and cook at 200°C for 5 minutes, turning halfway.
- Rest prawns for at least 5 minutes before serving with your favourite seafood sauce or a squeeze of lime.

CHEESEBURGER ONION RINGS

Mix your beef in a bowl with pepper and salt,
Slice onion rings – don't cry, it's not your fault!
Fill the rings with beef then add a piece of cheese,
Then top the onion rings with another piece of beef.
Dip the rings into the flour then dip into the egg,
Finally into the crumbs, then egg and crumbs again.
Cook the rings till golden brown and meat is fully cooked,
Dip them in tomato sauce ... admit it, now you're hooked.

Makes 8
500 g beef mince
1 teaspoon salt
1 teaspoon pepper
1 large onion
8 (2 cm) cubes tasty cheese
1 cup plain flour
3 eggs, beaten
2 cups panko breadcrumbs
cooking oil spray

- Add beef mince to a bowl with salt and pepper. Mix to combine, then separate the beef mixture into sixteen even pieces.
- Cut off both ends of the onion, peel it, then slice into three circular segments of an even width. Separate the segments into rings. Place eight onion rings onto a piece of baking paper.
- Place a piece of beef mixture into each of the rings and press flat. Push a piece of cheese into the centre of each, then top with another piece of beef and push it down flat.
- Preheat air fryer to 180°C.

- Place three bowls on the counter. Add flour to one bowl, beaten eggs to another and breadcrumbs to the last.
- Dip each ring into the flour, then egg, then breadcrumbs. Cover the ring completely at each stage. Then dip each ring back into the egg and the breadcrumbs again.
- Spray the air fryer basket with cooking oil spray and place half of the rings into the air fryer. Spray the rings with more cooking oil spray.
- Cook at 180°C for 10–12 minutes, turning halfway, until rings are golden and beef is cooked through. Repeat with remaining rings.
- Serve with tomato sauce and mustard.

PUMPKIN FRIES

Remove the skin and seeds, cut the pumpkin into fries,
Put them in a bowl and toss with spices to combine.
Add a touch of oil and toss the fries again,
Now they're ready to go in the air fryer, oh yeah!
Cook them for ten minutes at 160 degrees,
After five minutes give them a toss, pretty please?
Now your pumpkin fries are hot and good to eat,
Dip them in some sauce or serve them with some meat.

Serves 2–3
1 butternut pumpkin
1 teaspoon salt
1 teaspoon pepper
1 teaspoon paprika
¼ cup grated parmesan cheese
1 tablespoon olive oil

- Remove skin and seeds from pumpkin. Cut the pumpkin into 1 cm x 5 cm chips/fries.
- Place pumpkin fries into a large bowl and add salt, pepper, paprika and parmesan cheese. Toss well to coat. Add oil to the fries and toss again.
- Preheat air fryer to 160°C.
- Add fries to the air fryer basket and cook at 160°C for 10 minutes. Give the fries a shake, then cook at 200°C for a further 5 minutes or until golden.
- Serve with your favourite dipping sauce.

CRISPY CURRY DRUMSTICKS

Drizzle drumsticks with oil and give them a bit of a toss,
Combine the spices in a bowl then sprinkle them over the top.
Give them a shake, make sure the spices attach,
Put them in the air fryer – you can do them in one batch!
Twenty minutes to cook, turning them halfway,
Crispy curry drumsticks are on the menu today.

Makes 8
8 chicken drumsticks
1 tablespoon olive oil
1 teaspoon baking powder
1 teaspoon ground cumin
1 teaspoon ground coriander seeds
1 teaspoon turmeric
1 teaspoon paprika
½ teaspoon salt
½ teaspoon pepper

- Preheat air fryer to 200°C.
- Place the drumsticks and olive oil into a large bowl. Toss to coat.
- In a small bowl, combine baking powder, cumin, coriander seeds, turmeric, paprika, salt and pepper.
- Sprinkle the spice mixture over the drumsticks and toss well to coat.
- Place drumsticks into the air fryer in a single layer and cook at 200°C for 20 minutes, turning halfway, until chicken is crispy, golden and cooked through.

AIR FRIED SLIDERS

Cut your rolls in half so you've got two separate parts,
Add ham, tomato, spinach, cheese, to the bottom half.
Soften up some butter, add your spices and parmesan cheese,
Give it a good mix until it combines with ease.
Brush half of the mixture over the top of it,
Cover it with foil and cook it for a bit.
Take off the foil, brush on the rest of the mix,
Then cook for five more minutes and serve with hot chips.

Makes 8

8 dinner rolls (1 pack), connected
12–16 slices ham (1 pack)
2 tomatoes, sliced
60 g baby spinach
8 slices tasty cheese
150 g unsalted butter
4 garlic cloves, minced
½ teaspoon garlic salt
1 teaspoon Italian seasoning
¼ teaspoon paprika
½ teaspoon pepper
¼ cup grated parmesan cheese

- Preheat air fryer to 180°C.
- Keeping the dinner rolls connected to each other, cut in half, parallel to the counter, so that you have a top and bottom. *(Make sure your rolls will fit into the air fryer in one piece. If you have a small air fryer, split into two batches.)*

- Place the bottom half of the rolls onto a large piece of aluminium foil, then top with ham, tomato, baby spinach and cheese. Place the remaining part of the rolls on top and set aside. *(You don't have to use these exact ingredients as fillings, replace with whatever you like, but be sure to include the cheese!)*
- Add butter to a small bowl and soften in the microwave for 20–30 seconds. Once softened, add garlic, garlic salt, Italian seasoning, paprika, pepper and parmesan cheese. Stir until combined.
- Brush half of the butter mixture over the rolls, then cover with aluminium foil. Place rolls into the air fryer and cook for 7 minutes at 180°C. *(I like to add a few blobs of the garlic butter on top so its melts through the rolls.)*
- Remove rolls from the air fryer and remove the foil. Brush the remaining butter mixture over the rolls and place back into the air fryer uncovered. Cook for another 3–5 minutes or until golden.
- Tear rolls apart into individual sliders and serve.

♫ *Spray it with oil and cover it with foil* ♫

CARAMILK POPPERS

Break the chocolate into rows then place it on the pastry,
Cut around the chocolate, but be careful – don't be hasty.
Roll the pastry over and cut off extra bits,
Then use a little toothpick to poke some holes in it.
Brush them all with butter, including underneath,
Then put them in the air fryer – leave a small gap between.
Seven to ten minutes until pastry is golden brown,
Then serve them up with ice cream ... or just scoff them all down.

Makes 7–8
1 block Caramilk chocolate
2 sheets puff pastry, thawed
3 tablespoons butter, melted

- Break up chocolate into fingers/rows.
- Place puff pastry on a dry surface.
- Place the chocolate fingers onto the pastry, leaving enough space between each to be able to wrap it with pastry. Use a sharp knife to cut a rectangle around each chocolate finger. *(Each piece of pastry should be three times the width of the chocolate.)*
- Roll the pastry over the chocolate once, until the edges connect. Gently apply pressure to the pastry so that it seals in the chocolate. Squeeze the outside edges and cut off any excess pastry. Use a toothpick to poke three holes into each parcel. Repeat with remaining chocolates.
- Preheat air fryer to 200°C.
- Brush butter over pastries on all sides, including bottom.
- In batches, place the pastries into the air fryer in a single layer, leaving a small gap between each one.
- Cook at 200°C for 7–10 minutes or until pastry is golden brown.
- Let cool slightly before serving with a scoop of vanilla ice cream.

SMASHED SPROUTS

Cut off the tops and bottoms of the brussels sprouts,
Steam the sprouts till tender, then drain the sprouts out.
Add them to a bowl with oil and spices, then toss,
Then place them on a board and give them a good old squash!
Be careful not to break them – they need to stay intact,
Sprouts are better in an air fryer, that is just a fact.
Cook them for ten minutes until they are ready,
Then pair them with some protein and a side of spaghetti.

Serves 2–3
10 brussels sprouts
2 tablespoons olive oil
1 teaspoon garlic powder
1 teaspoon salt
1 teaspoon pepper

- Cut the tops and bottoms off brussels sprouts and remove any old outside leaves.
- Steam sprouts until tender. *(The easiest way to steam is to place them in a microwave-safe bowl with ¼ cup water, then cover and microwave on high for about 5 minutes.)*
- Preheat air fryer to 200°C.
- Drain sprouts and place into a large bowl. Add oil, garlic powder, salt and pepper and toss well to combine.
- Place sprouts onto a dry surface and apply pressure with the bottom of a drinking glass, squashing the sprouts to about half their original height.
- Place the smashed sprouts into the air fryer and cook at 200°C for 10 minutes or until crispy and golden.

COCONUT CHICKEN CHUNKS

Tenderise the chicken, bash it down a bunch,
Add a bit of seasoning then cut it into chunks.
Dip the chunks in flour, eggs, then coconut,
Now the chunks are ready, so heat the air fryer up.
Spray the fryer basket with a bit of oil spray,
Now air fry those chunks, turning them halfway.
When the chunks are ready they will look a treat,
Crunchy coconut chicken chunks that taste slightly sweet!

Serves 2
2 chicken breasts
pinch salt and pepper
½ cup plain flour
2 eggs, beaten
1 cup coconut flakes
cooking oil spray

- Place chicken breast onto a board and cover with cling wrap. Tenderise the breasts by hitting them with a meat tenderiser or a rolling pin until they are an even thickness. Season with salt and pepper.
- Cut the chicken into bite size cubes or chunks.
- Set three medium-sized bowls on the bench. Add flour to the first, beaten eggs to the second and coconut flakes to the third. (*If you have big coconut flakes, I recommend adding them to a ziplock bag and crushing them up a bit before you add them to the bowl.*)
- Preheat air fryer to 200°C.

- A few chunks at a time, dip the chicken into the flour, then the egg and then the coconut, making sure to completely cover the chicken at each step. Set aside and repeat with remaining chunks.
- Spray the air fryer basket with cooking oil spray and place the chicken chunks into the air fryer in a single layer, making sure they are not touching one another. You may have to cook them in batches.
- Cook at 200°C for 12–15 minutes, turning halfway, until golden and cooked through.
- Serve with your favourite dipping sauce.

♪ *Air fry some chicken. air fry your mum* ♪

BAKED POTATOES

Wash your potatoes, pat them dry,
Spray them with oil, give them some spice.
Rub the spice in – all over the sides,
Now they are ready to get air fried!
Cook for forty minutes, rotating halfway,
When pierced with a fork it should go in all the way.
Serve them alone with butter and chives,
Feed them to your kids, feed them to your wives.

Makes 2
2 medium brushed potatoes
cooking oil spray
½ teaspoon salt
½ teaspoon garlic powder

- Scrub and rinse your potatoes then pat dry with paper towel.
- Place potatoes into the air fryer and spray generously with cooking oil on all sides. Sprinkle with salt and garlic powder, rotating the potatoes as you go. Rub the salt into the potatoes with your hands so that they are fully coated.
- Cook at 200°C for 40 minutes, rotating halfway, until they are tender when you pierce with a fork.
- Serve with a tablespoon of butter and some chopped chives.

WAGON WHEEL PIES

Quarter the pastry then lay it on a board,
Top with Wagon Wheels and marshmallows, of course.
Firmly press the edges then seal with a fork,
Brush the pie with butter – make sure it's melted, you dork!
Air fry the pies at 200 degrees,
For eight to ten minutes – this is such a breeze.
Take the pies out when the pastry is golden brown,
Take a little bite, raise your hands, jump around.

Makes 4
2 sheets puff pastry, thawed
4 Wagon Wheels
8 marshmallows
2 tablespoons butter, melted

- Lay puff pastry on a dry surface and cut both sheets into quarters.
- Place a Wagon Wheel on top of four of the quarters. Top with 2 marshmallows on each Wagon Wheel. Place the remaining pastry quarters on top and firmly press around the edges to seal.
- Using the pointy end of a fork, firmly press around the edges of the pastry to seal further. Cut away any excess pastry and discard.
- Preheat air fryer to 200°C.
- Brush butter over all sides of the pies, including the bottom, then place pies into the air fryer.
- Cook at 200°C for 8–10 minutes or until pastry is golden and flaky.
- Serve immediately with ice cream.

CRAZY HACKS

Air fryers were originally marketed as a healthier alternative to deep frying. This is true in a sense, because an air fryer uses much less oil than traditional deep frying. Cooking healthy meals is great but it's also kind of boring. A big part of my channel is showcasing the weird and wonderful things you can create in an air fryer. Disrupting the general rules of cooking is extremely fun but also risky. I love taking risks.

In this chapter I will show you some oddly edible recipes that you can make in your air fryer that you might not have thought possible. Recipes such as Cheese and Bikkies Meatballs, Mac and Cheese Bread Bowls and the infamous Cookie Cake will get your imagination flowing and hopefully inspire you to start making your own odd creations in your air fryer.

JOY'S OPEN BREAKFAST SANDWICH

This was my very first viral TikTok recipe! I hate to admit it, but it wasn't even my idea ... it was my wife's! I sometimes wonder what would've been if I hadn't listened to my wife. Well for starters, I wouldn't be writing this book. Listen to your wives, folks!

Makes 2

2 slices bread
1½ tablespoons butter
2 eggs
2 rashers bacon
pepper to taste

- Preheat air fryer to 200°C.
- Place bread on a board. Use your fingers to press down in the centre of each slice to make an indent. Spread butter evenly over both sides of both pieces of bread.
- Remove basket from air fryer and set on a flat surface. Position both pieces of bread inside the basket. Crack eggs and drop into the indents. Place a rasher of bacon on top of each slice. (*The best part about this recipe is that you don't have to cook everything separately.*)
- Carefully reinsert basket into the air fryer. Cook at 200°C for 6–8 minutes or until the eggs and bacon are cooked through. (*Make sure to occasionally check the toast because the bacon can sometimes go flying around the air fryer like a kite in the wind.*)
- Season with pepper to taste and serve. (*Add a touch of BBQ sauce if you are a freak like me.*)

LEFTOVER BOMB!

This recipe is a sneaky way to spruce up your leftovers. You can basically use any leftovers you like, but for this example I'm using leftover butter chicken.

Makes 1

1 large bread roll
½ cup grated cheese
1 cup leftover butter chicken and rice
1 tablespoon butter, melted

- Preheat air fryer to 180°C.
- Using a bread knife, cut a wide, deep square into the top of the bread roll and remove the bread. Try to keep the offcut in one piece and set aside. *(Make sure you don't penetrate the bottom of the roll – you are basically making a bread bowl.)*
- Place half the grated cheese into the bottom of the bread roll.
- Preheat leftover butter chicken in the microwave until warm. Fill the bread roll with the warmed butter chicken until it almost reaches the top. *(You don't have to use butter chicken, you can use many different types of leftovers – pasta, taco filling, roast chicken – get experimenting!)*
- Brush butter over the outside of the roll and all over the offcut of bread.
- Top the roll with the remaining grated cheese. *(It's a good idea to firmly press the cheese into the butter chicken so it sticks and therefore won't fly around the air fryer.)*
- Place bread roll and offcut into the air fryer at 180°C for 5–7 minutes or until the cheese is melted and the roll is golden and toasty.

CHEESE AND BIKKIES MEATBALLS

It's an Australian tradition that upon arrival at any house party, the host will present you with a plate of cheese and bikkies, usually accompanied with some sliced meat or cabanossi. This is the pimped air fryer version!

Makes 10
500 g minced beef
1 teaspoon pepper
1 teaspoon paprika
200 g (10 individual portions) Babybel cheese
225 g Jatz crackers (1 box)
2 eggs, beaten
1 cup plain flour
cooking oil spray

- Add minced beef, pepper and paprika to a large bowl and combine.
- Remove cheese from wax packaging. *(I've added this step because a 'friend' of mine accidentally ate the wax packaging, thinking it was part of the cheese.)*
- Lay some baking paper onto a flat surface.
- Using your hands, make ten meatballs *(you don't have to be precise, roughly 50 g or ½ cup beef per ball)* and set them down onto the paper.
- Flatten each meatball to about 1 cm thickness and place a piece of cheese into the centre of each. Then wrap the meat around the cheese and enclose. *(The cheese should be in the centre of the meatball.)* Set aside.
- Place crackers into a ziplock bag and close, making sure there is no air left in the bag. Place the bag onto a flat surface and cover with a tea towel. Use a rolling pin to crush the crackers into small crumbs. Empty crumbs into a medium-sized bowl.

- Add beaten eggs to another medium-sized bowl and flour to a third.
- Preheat air fryer to 180°C.
- Roll each meatball in flour, shaking off any excess, then dip in egg and cover in crushed crackers.
- Spray the base of the air fryer basket with cooking spray and place half of the crumbed meatballs into the air fryer. Cook at 180°C for 10 minutes or until golden and cooked through, then repeat with remaining meatballs. *(If the cheese is oozing out, it's a good sign that the meatball is cooked.)*

♫ *I've got two favourite things in* ♫
this world. one of them is cheese.
the other one is dogs. ♪

TORTILLA CONES

Tacos are one of my favourite foods. But I've always found that more of the filling ends up on my shirt than in my mouth. These tortilla cones solve that problem.

Makes 4
4 medium tortillas
taco fillings (e.g. diced tomato, avocado, chicken, coriander)

- Preheat air fryer to 180°C.
- Lay a tortilla onto a chopping board. Using a knife, cut a line from the centre of the tortilla to the outside edge. Repeat with the remaining tortillas.
- Using your hands, move the cut edge of the tortilla into itself, making a cone shape. The cone should be quite tight with no hole at the bottom.
- Use a toothpick to pin the edges of the tortilla together. Press the pointy end of the toothpick through the outside edge into the middle of the cone then from the middle to the outside again, like a sewing a needle. Repeat with the remaining tortillas.
- Place tortillas into the air fryer and cook at 180°C for 5 minutes or until toasted.
- Add taco fillings of your choice and serve.

PEANUT BUTTER CHICKEN TENDERS

Peanut butter and chicken sounds like a weird combination until you try it!

Makes 8–10
½ cup crunchy peanut butter
1 tablespoon soy sauce
1 cup plain flour
1 cup panko breadcrumbs
500 g chicken tenderloins
cooking oil spray

- Add peanut butter and soy sauce to a medium-sized bowl and stir to combine.
- Add flour to another medium-sized bowl and breadcrumbs to a third bowl.
- Dip a tenderloin into the flour, brushing off any excess. Then dip into the peanut butter mixture, covering the entire tenderloin. Then cover in breadcrumbs. Set aside and repeat with remaining tenderloins.
- Preheat air fryer to 180°C.
- Spray the base of the air fryer basket with some cooking oil spray and place the tenderloins into the air fryer.
- Cook at 180°C for 7–10 minutes, turning halfway, until chicken is cooked through.

COOKIE CAKE

Yep, it's a giant cookie! You can use pre-made cookie dough or your favourite cookie dough recipe. For this example, I'll be using my world-famous chocolate chip cookie recipe (as voted by me).

Makes 1

1 cup plain flour
¼ teaspoon baking soda
¼ teaspoon salt
¼ cup unsalted butter, melted
½ cup brown sugar, packed
¼ cup white sugar
1 egg
½ tablespoon vanilla extract
1 cup chocolate chips

- In a medium-sized bowl, sift together flour, baking soda and salt. Set aside.
- In a large mixing bowl, mix the melted butter, brown sugar and white sugar until well combined and smooth. Add egg and vanilla then beat until you get a creamy texture. *(I like to use an electric hand mixer but you can do it by hand if you don't have one.)*
- Add the flour mixture to the wet mixture and fold together until just combined. Gently stir in the chocolate chips with a wooden spoon.
- Place a sheet of baking paper onto a chopping board. Remove air fryer basket from air fryer and set face down onto the paper. Use a sharp knife or scissors to cut the paper around the outside of the basket. Turn the basket around, place paper cutout inside and then back into the air fryer.

- Preheat air fryer to 160°C.
- Drop cookie dough onto the baking paper inside the air fryer basket and press down, spreading the dough evenly over the paper into a cake shape.
- Cook at 160°C for 15 minutes or until cooked through.
- Remove air fryer basket and let cookie cake cool inside the basket for a few minutes, then transfer onto a wire rack to cool completely.
- Serve in slices with cream or on its own.

♫ When I'm feeling stressed, anxious or depressed, I go and get myself some cookie dough. ♫

NO NURSE BACON

I love bacon. Like, love bacon! But before I had an air fryer, I rarely cooked bacon because it felt like a tedious task. Lots of cleaning up and fat spitting everywhere. You had to wait by the stove and nurse the bacon through the whole cooking process. Cooking bacon in the air fryer changes that. This isn't so much a recipe as it is a new technique.

Serves 2–4

200 g streaky bacon rashers

- Preheat air fryer to 180°C.
- Lay bacon down inside the air fryer basket.
- Cook at 180°C and walk away for 8–15 minutes, depending on how crispy you like it *(refer to the timing guide below. There is no need to flip or poke or prod your bacon. The air fryer will do the job for you.)*

Timing Guide:

8 minutes for chewy bacon
12 minutes for semi-crispy bacon
15 minutes for super-crispy bacon

These are just guidelines. Everyone likes their bacon cooked differently. So, the first time you cook bacon in the air fryer, make sure you note how long it takes to reach your desired crispiness. Then next time you can just set the timer and go about your morning routine.

MEXICAN LASAGNE

Not technically lasagne, but technically easy and delicious.

Serves 1–2

3 small flour tortillas
½ cup salsa
⅓ cup grated cheese
125 g can black beans, rinsed

- Preheat air fryer to 180°C.
- Place a tortilla onto a dry surface. Spoon ⅓ of the salsa on top and spread over the tortilla, covering it. Place half the black beans on top and then sprinkle half the cheese evenly on top.
- Place another tortilla on top of the cheese, top with ⅓ salsa, the remaining black beans and cheese.
- Top with the last tortilla. Spread the remaining salsa over the top.
- Secure the tortillas together with a couple of toothpicks. *(This will stop the top tortilla from flying around the air fryer.)*
- Air fry at 180°C for 10 minutes or until cheese is oozing out and the lasagne is heated through.
- Slice and serve.

LEFTOVER MAC AND CHEESE SAUSAGES

I always make way too much mac and cheese. I think it's because, deep down, I want leftovers. These mac and cheese sausages are a super fun way to turn those leftovers into a main meal.

Makes 4

2 cups leftover mac and cheese (it doesn't have to be leftover, you can always make it specifically for this recipe)
2 eggs, beaten
1 cup plain flour
1 cup panko breadcrumbs
cooking oil spray

- Lay a sheet of cling wrap onto a flat surface. Place ½ cup of cold mac and cheese into the centre of the cling wrap. Fold the cling wrap over the mac and cheese and roll into a sausage shape, making sure the cling wrap is tightly secured. Twist the ends of the cling wrap to make it even tighter. Set aside and repeat with the remaining mac and cheese until you have four sausages.
- Put the sausages into the freezer for 30 minutes. *(You don't want to completely freeze them but they will need to be almost frozen so that they stay in shape for the next step.)*
- Meanwhile, add beaten eggs to a medium-sized bowl, flour to another and breadcrumbs to a third.
- Preheat air fryer to 180°C.
- Remove sausages from freezer and gently unwrap them. *(If they fall apart when you are unwrapping them, wrap them back up and put them back into the freezer until they are firm.)*

- Dip an unwrapped sausage into the flour and cover, shaking off any excess. Then dip in the egg, covering completely before covering with breadcrumbs. Dip the crumbed sausage back into the egg and then crumb again. Repeat with remaining sausages. *(The double crumb will help the sausage keep its shape through the cooking process.)*
- Lightly spray the air fryer basket with cooking oil spray and place sausages into the air fryer. Give the sausages another light spray.
- Cook at 180°C for 12–15 minutes or until golden and heated through.

MASSAMAN VEAL SCHNITZEL

There are hundreds of ways to spruce up a schnitzel. This schnitzel is inspired by my favourite Thai dish: Massaman Curry.

Makes 2
2 veal sizzle steaks/schnitzels
1 cup plain flour
1 cup panko breadcrumbs
2 tablespoons massaman curry paste
1 cup light coconut milk
cooking oil spray

- Place veal steaks onto a piece of baking paper and cover with cling wrap. Using a meat tenderising hammer, gently tenderise the veal by hammering it. It should flatten out easily.
- Add flour to a medium-sized bowl and breadcrumbs to another bowl. In a third bowl, add 1 tablespoon massaman curry paste and ½ cup coconut milk. Stir until combined.
- Add veal to the flour and cover completely. Shake off any excess flour then drench the veal in the massaman mixture. Once fully covered, dip the veal into the breadcrumbs, covering completely. Set aside and repeat with the second piece of veal.
- Preheat air fryer to 180°C.
- Spray the air fryer basket with cooking oil spray and carefully place the veal schnitzels into the air fryer.
- Spray the schnitzels with some more cooking oil spray and cook for 5–7 minutes, turning halfway. Schnitzels should be golden brown and cooked through.
- While the schnitzels are cooking, add the remaining massaman paste and coconut milk to a bowl and mix to combine. Heat the mixture in the microwave on high for 2 minutes or until sauce thickens slightly.
- Serve schnitzels with massaman sauce.

CHEESY SAUSAGE BOYS

This was one of the first recipes I created when I was a kid. I guess I'm still a big kid at heart.

Makes 6
6 thick sausages
6 cheese stringers
1 cup plain flour
2 eggs, beaten
1 cup panko breadcrumbs

- Place sausages onto a dry surface.
- Use a sharp knife to slice the sausages lengthwise but be careful not to cut through the entire sausage. *(The easiest way to describe how to do this is to cut the sausage like you would a hot dog bun. Imagine that the sausage is the bun and the cheese is the hot dog.)*
- Remove the plastic wrap from the cheese stringers *(very important, LOL)*. Place a cheese stringer into a sausage and press firmly to engulf the cheese inside. Repeat with remaining sausages and cheese. *(Sometimes I use a toothpick to keep the sausage intact for better presentation.)*
- Place three medium-sized bowls onto the kitchen bench. Add flour to the first, eggs to the second and breadcrumbs to the third.
- Dip the cheese-filled sausage into the flour and cover completely. Shake off any excess flour then drench in the egg before completely covering in breadcrumbs. Repeat with remaining sausages.
- Preheat air fryer to 180°C.
- Place the sausages into the air fryer in a single layer and cook at 180°C for 8–12 minutes or until golden and cheese is melted and oozing.

NATE'S LEFTOVER SPAG BOL SPRING ROLLS

My nephew Nate loves spaghetti bolognaise. He would eat it for every meal if he was allowed to. This recipe is for him.

Makes 8

1 cup leftover spaghetti bolognaise
⅓ cup grated cheese
8 spring roll wrappers, thawed
cooking oil spray

- Place spaghetti bolognaise and cheese onto a chopping board. (*This recipe works better with leftover spaghetti bolognaise because it has been chilled in the fridge and should be firm. You can make these spring rolls with freshly cooked spaghetti bolognaise but make sure to chill it first*). Use a sharp knife to chop the spaghetti into small pieces until it is fully combined with the cheese.
- On a dry surface, place a spring roll wrapper (*smooth side down*) in a diamond position. Place a heaped dessertspoon of spaghetti filling on the bottom corner of the wrapper. Roll the wrapper up halfway, fold sides in, then keep rolling rolling. Dip your finger into some water and lightly moisten the last flap of the wrapper. Finish rolling and slightly press along the seal until it sticks. Repeat with the remaining wrappers.
- Spray both sides of spring rolls with a generous amount of cooking oil spray.
- Preheat air fryer to 190°C.
- Place spring rolls into the air fryer and cook at 190°C for 7–10 minutes or until the pastry is golden and crunchy.
- Serve immediately. (*You will want to eat these as fast as possible because if my nephew Nate finds out you have them, he will find you and he will eat them, LOL.*)

BANANARAMAS

This is a super simple way to spruce up your bananas. I considered naming this recipe Bananas in Pyjamas, but these bananas are barely dressed!

Makes enough for 2
2 ripe bananas, cut in half
1 tablespoon butter, melted
¼ tablespoon cinnamon
½ teaspoon brown sugar

- Put your bananas into a bowl. *(You can cut your bananas any way you like. I prefer half because I can eat them with my hands, but you can cut into quarters or even slices.)* Add butter, cinnamon and brown sugar and mix until the bananas are covered evenly.
- Preheat air fryer at 190°C for 3 minutes.
- Place a piece of aluminium foil on the base of the air fryer, making sure to leave some of the holes in the basket exposed *(this will help with the clean up)*. Place bananas on top of the foil, making sure none overlap and cook them at 190°C for 5 minutes. Flip bananas over and cook for a further 3 minutes or until caramelised.
- Eat the bananas as they are, with ice cream, or on toast.

GLAZED DOUGHNUTS

A healthy doughnut? There is such a thing!

Makes 10–12
Doughnuts
1 cup milk, lukewarm
¼ cup granulated sugar
2 teaspoons active dry yeast
1 egg
½ teaspoon salt
3 cups plain flour
¼ cup unsalted butter, melted
cooking oil spray

Glaze
2 cups icing sugar
¼ cup milk
1 teaspoon vanilla extract

- In a large bowl, gently mix milk, 1 teaspoon sugar and yeast. Let sit for 10 minutes until it becomes foamy. *(If nothing happens, your milk was too hot – so start over.)*
- Add remaining sugar, egg, salt, 2 cups flour and butter to the milk mixture. Mix on low speed using an electric mixer until combined. Keep mixing while gradually adding the remaining flour until the dough doesn't stick to the bowl. Increase speed to medium–low for 5 minutes, until the dough is smooth and stretchy. *(If you don't have an electric mixer, you can knead it by hand but it will take time and you may break a sweat.)*
- Put the dough into a greased bowl and cover with cling wrap. Let the dough rise until it's doubled in size. *(This will take 30–60 minutes. You can test the dough by making a dent with your finger. If the dent doesn't pop back, it's ready).*

- Place the dough onto a floured surface, push it down and gently roll it out to about 1½ cm thick. Cut out 10–12 doughnuts using a cookie cutter and remove the centre of each doughnut with a smaller cookie cutter.
- Place doughnuts *(and the doughnut holes!)* onto baking paper and softly cover with cling wrap, leaving enough space between each for them to double in size. Let the doughnuts rise until doubled in size *(around 30 minutes).*
- Preheat air fryer to 180°C.
- Spray air fryer basket with cooking oil spray and transfer doughnuts to air fryer in a single layer *(you will have to cook them in batches).* Spray doughnuts with cooking oil spray and cook at 180°C for 4 minutes or until golden brown. Repeat with the remaining doughnuts and holes.
- While the doughnuts are cooking, whisk together icing sugar, milk and vanilla extract to form a smooth glaze.
- Dip hot doughnuts and doughnut holes into the glaze, using a fork to submerge them. Place on a wire rack and let sit until glaze hardens. This should take about 10 minutes. *(I like to place a sheet of baking paper underneath the rack to catch the drips.)*
- Enjoy!

Let's make a giant doughnut. why not? It's a doughnut!

SALADA PIZZAS

This recipe was created out of pure laziness but ended up being truly delicious! I can almost hear the Italians screaming profanities at me!

Makes 2
2 square Salada crackers (the big ones)
2 tablespoons pizza sauce
8 slices pepperoni
⅓ cup grated cheese

- Preheat air fryer to 200°C.
- Place Salada crackers onto a dry surface. Add a tablespoon of pizza sauce to each and spread evenly over the cracker, covering it completely.
- Place 4 slices of pepperoni onto each cracker then cover with grated cheese.
- Carefully place the pizzas into the air fryer and cook at 200°C for 3–5 minutes or until the cheese is melted. *(Grated cheese can sometimes fly off the pizza in the air fryer, making a huge mess. The best way to counteract this is to check on the pizza every 30 seconds for the first couple of minutes. If the cheese has moved, collect it and place it back onto the pizza. Once the cheese starts to soften it will stay in place.)*

MAC AND CHEESE BREAD BOWLS

As a kid, I always thought it would be cool if someone would make a bowl you could eat. I am now that someone.

Makes 2
300 g elbow macaroni
¼ cup butter, plus extra for spreading
¼ cup plain flour
½ teaspoon salt
pepper to taste
2 cups milk
2 cups grated cheese
1 loaf unsliced white bread

- Bring a large pot of water to the boil. Add macaroni and cook until firm to the bite – about 8 minutes. Drain.
- Melt butter in a saucepan over medium heat. Stir in flour, salt and pepper until smooth. Slowly add the milk to the pan stirring continuously until mixture is smooth and bubbling. Add the cheese and stir until incorporated. Remove from the heat and mix in the macaroni.
- Cut the loaf of bread into thirds. *(Save the middle third for later, as we will only be using the two end pieces).* Turn the two end pieces soft side up and scoop out the bread inside, leaving the crust intact. Spread some butter around the outside of the bread bowls.
- Place the bread bowls into the air fryer and cook at 200°C for 3–5 minutes or until the bread is golden and toasted.
- Fill bread bowls with mac and cheese and serve.

♪ *I want a bowl, a bowl that you can eat, yeah!* ♪

CHEETOS BACON

Bacon is usually regarded as a breakfast food. This is more of an afternoon delight.

Makes 6
90 g (1 bag) Cheetos Cheese and Bacon Balls
½ cup plain flour
1 egg, beaten
6 rashers streaky bacon

- Empty Cheetos into a ziplock bag. Push out any excess air and seal. Use your hand to crush Cheetos into small crumbs and add to a bowl.
- Add flour to another bowl and beaten egg to a third.
- Dip bacon into flour and cover. Shake off excess flour then dip into egg. Remove bacon from egg wash and dip into Cheetos crumbs, completely covering the bacon. Repeat with remaining bacon and set aside.
- Preheat air fryer to 200°C.
- Add bacon to air fryer in a single layer and cook at 200°C for 7–10 minutes or until crispy and golden. *(You can cook the bacon for longer if you want it super crispy.)*
- Place bacon on a paper towel-lined plate and rest for a few minutes, then serve.

SAUSAGE SIZZLE POCKETS

The Australian version of pizza pockets.

Makes 4
4 thin sausages
8 slices bread
2 tablespoons tomato sauce
2 tablespoons mustard
½ cup grated cheese
2 tablespoons butter, melted

- Preheat air fryer to 180°C.
- Place sausages into the air fryer and cook at 180°C for 8 minutes or until cooked through, turning halfway.
- Meanwhile, cut the crusts off the bread and discard.
- Remove cooked sausages from air fryer and cut into halves.
- Increase temperature in air fryer to 200°C.
- Place four slices of crustless bread onto a dry surface. Place two sausage halves on top of each slice. Top evenly with tomato sauce, mustard and cheese. Place the remaining four slices of bread on top.
- Use your finger to seal the outside edges of the bread by firmly pressing down. Then use your thumb and index finger to pinch the edges and secure further. Brush both sides of each pocket with melted butter.
- Add pockets to the air fryer and cook at 200°C for 5 minutes or until toasted and golden.

THE WORLD'S EASIEST QUESADILLA

As voted by me!

Makes 1
2 flour tortillas
⅓ roast chicken, shredded
¼ cup black beans
⅓ cup grated cheese
1 tablespoon hot sauce
1 tablespoon butter

- Remove basket from air fryer.
- Lay a flour tortilla down flat inside the air fryer basket. Top with chicken, beans and cheese, covering the tortilla evenly. Drizzle with hot sauce.
- Spread butter over one side of the remaining tortilla then place it, butter side up, on top of the other tortilla. Secure using a few toothpicks. *(Stick the toothpicks directly through both tortillas to stop the top tortilla from moving during the cooking process.)*
- Reinsert basket back into air fryer and cook tortilla at 200°C for 5–7 minutes, or until golden and the cheese is melted.
- Cut into quarters and serve.

PICKLE POPPERS

Don't underestimate the power of a pickle.

Makes 4
4 large pickles
4 slices Swiss cheese
4 slices salami
½ cup plain flour
2 eggs, beaten
1 cup panko breadcrumbs
cooking oil spray

- Cut pickles in half, lengthwise. Lay four of the halves down onto a dry surface, flat side up.
- Fold cheese slices in half and place on top of the pickles.
- Roll up the slices of salami and place on top of the cheese. Top with remaining pickle halves and secure with a toothpick. *(You could stop here and enjoy the pickles as they are, but if you are a risk taker, follow the next steps.)*
- Preheat air fryer to 180°C.
- Add beaten eggs to a small bowl, flour to another and breadcrumbs to a third.
- Dip a pickle popper into the flour, shaking off any excess. Then submerge in the egg, making sure to cover the entire pickle so there are no dry bits. Then dip into breadcrumbs and completely cover the pickle. Dip the crumbed pickle popper back into the egg, then back into the breadcrumbs. *(This will make the pickle extra crunchy.)* Repeat with remaining pickles.
- Spray the base of the preheated air fryer with cooking oil spray. Place the pickles into the air fryer and spray with some more cooking oil spray.
- Cook at 180°C for 10 minutes, turning halfway, until golden and the cheese is oozing.

Have you ever stumbled upon a flavour combination that sounds ridiculous but tastes amazing? I'm not talking about toothpaste and orange juice, I'm talking about peanut butter and pickles, or ice cream and French fries, or even bananas and cheese. Sometimes the foods that sound weird when put together, actually taste amazing. In this chapter you will find some odd combinations to devour such as Zucchini Doritos Fries, Big Mac Spring Rolls and the super yummy Dessert Nachos!

STICKY BACON

I'm salivating at the thought of this recipe! You could almost classify it as a dessert.

Makes enough for 2–4
¼ cup brown sugar
¼ teaspoon pepper
⅛ teaspoon sweet paprika
200 g middle bacon rashers

- Preheat air fryer to 180°C.
- In a small bowl, combine brown sugar, pepper and paprika together.
- Place bacon inside the air fryer. *(Make sure not to crowd the air fryer too much. A single layer of bacon will work perfectly).* Sprinkle the bacon with half of the sugar mixture and spread it over the bacon *(I like to use the back of a spoon)*, covering the pieces evenly.
- Cook bacon at 180°C for 8 minutes then flip and add the remaining sugar mix to the other side of the bacon. Cook for 7 more minutes.
- Once cooked, move the bacon to a cooling rack and rest for about 5 minutes. *(This step is important because the bacon will become super sticky when it cools. You will be cleaning your air fryer for hours if you miss this step.)*
- Serve as a side with eggs or as a snack.

ZUCCHINI DORITOS FRIES

Zucchini fries are super healthy. These zucchini fries are not as healthy, but taste way better. Ying and yang, baby!

Serves 2

2 medium zucchinis
60 g (1 small bag) Doritos cheese supreme corn chips
½ cup parmesan cheese, grated
½ cup plain flour
2 eggs, beaten
cooking oil spray

- Cut the zucchini lengthwise into sticks about 1 cm thick and 10 cm long. *(They should look like fries.)*
- Place Doritos into a sealed bag, making sure there is no air in the bag. Lay the bag onto a flat surface and cover with a tea towel. Using the base of your fist *(or a meat tenderiser, or anything solid that won't break)*, press down onto the Doritos, crushing them into tiny crumbs. Add to a shallow bowl with parmesan cheese.
- Add flour to another shallow bowl and beaten eggs to a third.
- Dip zucchini fries into the flour and shake off excess. Then dip into the egg, then Doritos mix, making sure the fries are fully coated in each. *(If you want a really thick coating, you can re-dip into the egg and Doritos mix again.)*
- Preheat air fryer to 200°C.
- Generously spray zucchini fries with cooking oil spray.
- Working in batches, place the fries in a single layer in the air fryer and cook for 10 minutes at 200°C, turning halfway, until golden and crispy.

SWEET AND SPICY CHICKEN THUMBS

I lived in LA for a few years, back when I was a budding musician. I ate at many different places, from fancy restaurants to food trucks but none more memorable that Roscoe's Chicken and Waffles! Their specialty is waffles, topped with fried chicken, hot sauce and maple syrup. At first, I thought the combination was ridiculous, but once I tried it, I was hooked. This recipe is inspired by that experience.

Makes 8–10
500 g chicken tenderloins
¼ cup sriracha hot sauce
½ teaspoon salt
½ teaspoon pepper
1 cup Kellogg's Crunchy Nut Cornflakes
2 eggs, beaten
1 cup plain flour

- In a medium-sized bowl, combine chicken tenderloins, sriracha, salt and pepper. *(If you want it really spicy you can add more sriracha, but this amount compliments the sweetness.)*
- Add Crunchy Nut Cornflakes to a ziplock bag. *(You can also use frosted flakes but I don't recommend using regular corn flakes as they aren't sweet enough.)* Place bag onto a hard flat surface and cover with a tea towel. Using a rolling pin *(or even a mug)*, apply pressure to the cornflakes, crushing them into crumbs.
- In three separate bowls, add cornflake crumbs, beaten eggs and flour.

- Preheat air fryer to 180°C.
- One by one, dip the sriracha covered chicken into the flour, shaking off any excess. Then dip into the egg and crumbs, covering completely at each stage. Set aside and repeat with remaining chicken.
- Place chicken into the preheated air fryer and cook at 180°C for about 10–12 minutes, flipping halfway, or until the chicken is cooked through and golden brown.
- Serve immediately. (*I like to dip them in maple syrup for extra sweetness.*)

Crumb it like you mean it

BIG MAC SPRING ROLLS

These little treats are a staple at my house. The only issue is that they don't last very long because they are so delicious!

Makes 8

2 hamburger patties (you can make them yourself or buy them pre-made)

¼ cup pickles, diced

½ cup cheese, grated

½ onion, diced

½ tablespoon sesame seeds

¼ cup special burger sauce, plus more for dipping (I can't believe they sell this in supermarkets now!)

salt and pepper to taste

8 spring roll wrappers, thawed

cooking oil spray

- Preheat air fryer to 190°C.
- Place burger patties into air fryer and cook at 190°C for 8 minutes, turning halfway.
- Remove patties from air fryer and let cool for 15 minutes. *(If you want to speed up this process, just put the cooked patties into the fridge.)*
- Once patties are cooled, place onto a chopping board and dice into small pieces.
- In a large bowl, add chopped patties, pickles, cheese, onion, sesame seeds and burger sauce. Combine well. Add salt and pepper to taste.

- On a dry surface, place the wrappers smooth side down in a diamond position. Place a heaped dessertspoon of burger filling in the bottom corner. Roll up halfway, fold sides in, then finish rolling. Dip your finger into some water and lightly moisten the last flap of the wrapper. Lightly press along the seal until it sticks. Repeat with the remaining wrappers.
- Spray both sides of spring rolls with a generous amount of cooking oil spray.
- Place spring rolls into the air fryer and cook at 190°C for 7–10 minutes or until the pastry is golden and crunchy.
- Serve with special burger dipping sauce.

BACON-WRAPPED AVOCADO WEDGES

Bacon and avocado is a combination I love! These little bite-sized snacks are a great appetiser. Super simple and quick!

Makes 8
1 avocado
200 g streaky bacon rashers

- Preheat air fryer to 200°C.
- Halve avocado, remove pit and peel.
- Cut avocado into eight wedges.
- Gently wrap a rasher of bacon around each avocado wedge and place into the air fryer. (*You can use a toothpick to hold the bacon in place.*)
- Cook at 200°C for 10 minutes.

♪ Here's a snack that'll fill the gap and it won't cost you a lot ♪

EGGVOCADO

Here is another simple avocado recipe. It's a great low-carb breakfast, but also amazing on toast!

Makes 2
1 avocado
2 eggs
¼ teaspoon sweet paprika
salt and pepper to taste

- Preheat air fryer to 200°C.
- Halve avocado, remove pit and peel.
- Place both halves into the air fryer with the pit hole facing upwards. *(I like to slightly flatten the underside of the avocado by slicing off a smidge so that it doesn't wobble around.)*
- Crack an egg into each hole.
- Air fry at 200°C for 5 minutes or until the egg is cooked but the yolk is still runny.
- Sprinkle with paprika, salt and pepper and serve as they are or on buttered toast.

EGG CUPCAKES

A fun, colourful way to eat eggs!

Makes 4
4 eggs
½ teaspoon salt
½ teaspoon pepper
cooking oil spray
1 tomato, diced
½ red onion, diced
¼ bunch fresh parsley
1 avocado, pitted and peeled
½ cup cooked, chopped bacon pieces

- Crack eggs into a bowl. Season with salt and pepper and whisk well. Each cupcake is one egg which is about a quarter of a cup. *(You should have about one cup of egg mixture.)*
- Spray some non-stick patty pans with cooking oil spray. *(I like to use silicone patty pans because they rarely stick at all.)*
- Preheat air fryer to 180°C for 3 minutes.
- Divide the egg mixture, tomato, onion and parsley between four patty pans.
- Place cupcakes into air fryer at 180°C for 5–7 minutes or until the egg is fully cooked.
- Meanwhile, in a small bowl, use a fork to mash the avocado. *(If you want to save washing up, you can mash the avocado inside the avocado skin.)*
- Once cooked and while still hot, spread the avocado over the top of each cupcake so it resembles icing. Top with a sprinkle of bacon pieces and serve warm.

CADBURY FAVOURITES PASTRY SLICE

Turn a regular box of Cadbury Favourites into gooey chocolate-filled pastry.

Serves 4

2 sheets puff pastry, thawed

8 miniature chocolates from a box of Cadbury Favourites (My choices would be Picnic, Cherry Ripe, Boost, Dairy Milk, Moro, Dream, Crunchie and Flake)

1 tablespoon butter, melted

- Lay a sheet of baking paper onto a board and place one sheet of pastry on top.
- Unwrap eight of your favourite chocolates and place them on the pastry in two rows. Leave a 1 cm gap between each chocolate.
- Brush some of the butter around the outside of the chocolates.
- Lay the remaining piece of pastry over the top of the chocolates, then using a chopstick *(or the handle of a butter knife)*, press down firmly between chocolates, sticking the top layer of pastry to the bottom layer.
- Cut the excess pastry, leaving about 2 cm around the perimeter *(you are making just one big slice, not individual pastries)*. Use your fingers to seal the edges, then use a fork to connect further, making little indents. Brush the remaining butter over the top of the slice.
- Preheat air fryer to 200°C.
- Place slice into air fryer and cook at 200°C for 8–10 minutes or until the pastry is golden.
- Let cool for 5 minutes then cut into four pieces and serve warm.

STRAWBERRY JAM STRAWS

I make these when I run out of sweets. You only need a few ingredients and they are really easy to make. Well, easier than getting dressed and going to the shop to buy ice cream.

Makes 15–20
1 egg
3 tablespoons sugar
½ teaspoon cinnamon
2 sheets puff pastry
⅓ cup strawberry jam

- Preheat air fryer to 200°C.
- In a small bowl, whisk the egg. *(I like to add a tablespoon of water to the egg mixture to thin it out slightly.)*
- In another small bowl, add sugar and cinnamon then mix to combine.
- On a lightly floured surface, slightly flatten both sheets of pastry with a rolling pin. Spread the jam evenly over one sheet of pastry, leaving about a 1 cm space around the edges. Brush the uncovered edges with egg wash and place second sheet of pastry on top. Press firmly around the edges to seal.
- Brush the top sheet of pastry with egg wash and sprinkle evenly with cinnamon sugar.
- Use a sharp knife *(or a pizza cutter)* to cut the dough into 1½ cm strips. Twist the strips a few times until they look like straws.
- In batches, place straws into the air fryer *(leave a 2 cm gap between each)* and cook at 200°C for 10 minutes, turning halfway, until golden brown and crisp.
- Rest for 5 minutes and serve. *(Perfect with a dollop of cream.)*

APPLE PIE SPRING ROLLS

Sweet and crunchy rolls of wholesome goodness.

Makes 8

8 spring roll wrappers, thawed
200 g apple cinnamon pie filling (you can make the filling from
  scratch if you want but I'm lazy)
cooking oil spray

- Preheat air fryer to 190°C.
- On a dry surface, place the wrappers smooth side down in a
  diamond position. Place a heaped dessertspoon of apple pie filling
  onto the bottom corner. Roll up halfway, fold sides in, then finish
  rolling. Dip your finger into some water and lightly moisten the last
  flap of the wrapper, slightly pressing along the seal until it sticks.
  Repeat with the remaining wrappers.
- Spray both sides of spring rolls with a generous amount of cooking
  oil spray.
- Place spring rolls into the air fryer and cook at 190°C for
  7–10 minutes or until the pastry is golden and crunchy.

DESSERT NACHOS

Nachos as a dessert? Yes please! This sweet version of nachos will knock your socks off! My favourite toppings are banana, chocolate and whipped cream, but you can use any sweet toppings you like.

Serves 2–3
Nachos Chips
3 flour tortillas
3 tablespoons butter, melted
3 teaspoons sugar
½ teaspoon cinnamon
cooking oil spray

Toppings
1 banana, sliced
¼ cup chocolate sauce
whipped cream

- Lay tortillas on a flat surface. Brush with butter.
- In a small bowl, add sugar and cinnamon then mix to combine. Sprinkle the cinnamon sugar evenly over the tortillas. *(You only need to cover one side of the tortillas, but if you are looking for extra sweetness, you can flip them and coat the other side in butter and cinnamon sugar, too.)*
- Use a pizza cutter or a sharp knife to cut the tortillas into wedges. *(I like to cut my tortillas into sixteen wedges per tortilla, but you can cut them any size you prefer.)*
- Preheat air fryer to 170°C.

- Spray the base of your air fryer with cooking oil spray, then add a single layer of chips. *(You will have to do them in batches as you want the hot air pushing around the air fryer for extra crispy chips.)*
- Air fry at 170°C for 5–6 minutes. Repeat with remaining batches.
- Add chips to a bowl and top with banana, chocolate sauce and whipped cream, or sweet toppings of your choice. *(You can use anything you have available such as berries, nuts, caramel sauce, biscuits … the options are endless.)*

There's nothing better than a banana
in and around your mouth

VEAL PIZZA PARMI

What do you get when you cross a parmi with a pizza?

Makes 2
2 veal sizzle steaks/schnitzels
1 cup plain flour
1 cup panko breadcrumbs
1 egg, beaten
cooking oil spray
2 tablespoons pizza sauce
8 slices pepperoni
100 g bocconcini cheese

- Place veal steaks onto a piece of baking paper and cover with cling wrap. Using a meat tenderising hammer, gently tenderise the veal by hammering it. It should flatten out easily.
- Add flour, breadcrumbs and beaten egg to three separate bowls.
- Add veal to the flour and cover completely. Shake off any excess then drench in the egg. Once fully covered, dip the veal into the breadcrumbs, covering completely. Set aside and repeat with the second piece of veal.
- Preheat air fryer to 180°C.
- Spray the air fryer basket with cooking oil spray and carefully place the veal schnitzels into the air fryer.
- Spray the schnitzels with some more cooking oil spray and cook for 5–7 minutes, turning halfway. Schnitzels should be golden brown and cooked through.
- Remove schnitzels from air fryer and increase temperature to 200°C. Spread 1 tablespoon pizza sauce evenly over each schnitzel. Top with pepperoni then tear the bocconcini in halves and place on top.
- Return schnitzels to air fryer and cook at 200°C for 2–3 minutes, or until the cheese has melted.

VEGEMITE CHICKEN WINGS

Chicken wings are one of the easiest things to cook in an air fryer. They come out so crispy! This recipe uses the saltiness of Vegemite to bring out a flavour in the chicken that you probably haven't tried before.

Makes 8–12

cooking oil spray
8–12 chicken wings
2 teaspoons Vegemite
⅓ cup boiling water
2 tablespoons sweet chilli sauce
2 tablespoons oyster sauce
2 tablespoons brown sugar
2 tablespoons rice wine vinegar
1 tablespoon sesame oil (or you can use olive oil)
3 gloves garlic, finely chopped

- Preheat air fryer to 180°C.
- Spray the base of the air fryer basket with cooking oil spray and place the chicken wings into air fryer. Spray with some more cooking oil spray. Cook wings for 7 minutes or until almost cooked through, turning halfway.
- Meanwhile, combine Vegemite and boiling water in a small bowl until smooth. Stir in sweet chilli sauce, oyster sauce, brown sugar and vinegar.
- Heat sesame oil in a large frypan over medium heat and add chopped garlic and cook for 1 minute or until fragrant. Add Vegemite mixture and bring to a simmer. Simmer, covered, for 10 minutes.
- Remove chicken wings from air fryer and add to the frypan, covering the chicken with the Vegemite mixture. Simmer, uncovered, turning the chicken occasionally, for 5 minutes or until the chicken is cooked through and the sauce is sticky.
- Serve with steamed rice and vegetables.

CRUMBED CHEESE AND VEGEMITE SANDWICH

Cheese and Vegemite sandwiches are perfect. Why on earth would you crumb one? I guess you will have to try it to see for yourself.

Makes 1
2 slices bread
1 teaspoon butter
½ teaspoon Vegemite (or as much as you prefer, everybody is
    different)
1 slice tasty cheese
1 slice Swiss cheese
1 egg, beaten
⅓ cup plain flour
½ cup panko breadcrumbs
cooking oil spray

- Place bread onto a flat surface. Spread butter and Vegemite evenly over one side of each slice. Lay both pieces of cheese onto one of the slices of bread. *(Make sure you cover the entire piece of bread. If the bread is bigger than the slices of cheese, break them into pieces so you get full coverage.)* Place the remaining piece of bread butter side down on top of the cheese-topped bread.
- Add the flour to a medium-sized bowl, beaten egg to another and breadcrumbs to a third.

- Dip sandwich into the flour until covered *(make sure you cover the outside edges to seal in the cheese)*. Shake off excess flour then dip into the egg, then into the breadcrumbs. *(The sandwich should be completely sealed, so you shouldn't be able to see any cheese sticking out of the sandwich. The idea is to keep the cheese inside the sandwich so it doesn't all ooze out in the cooking process.)*
- Preheat air fryer to 180°C.
- Spay the base of the air fryer basket with cooking oil spray and place sandwich into air fryer.
- Cook at 180°C for 10 minutes, flipping halfway. The sandwich should be golden brown. *(If a little bit of cheese is oozing out it's a good sign it's ready.)*
- Slice and serve.

CHICKEN PESTO LASAGNE POCKETS

When I was growing up, my dad loved taking me to the bakery after school to get a pie. He would make me promise not to tell my mum. When we would get home, mum would always have an amazing dinner ready for us – often a mean pesto lasagne. This recipe is a sneaky way of bringing those dishes together.

Makes 4
6 fresh lasagne sheets
2 cups chopped cooked chicken
4 tablespoons basil pesto
200 ml light thickened cream
100 g grated parmesan cheese, plus extra to serve
salt and pepper to taste
2 sheets puff pastry, partially thawed
1 egg, beaten
roasted cherry tomatoes to serve

- Cut lasagne sheets in half and place in a heat proof dish. Cover with boiling water and allow to soften for 2 minutes. Move lasagne sheets to a tray and cover with cold water to refresh. Drain dish and pat sheets dry with a clean towel. Cut the lasagne sheets into 10 cm squares.
- Combine the chicken, pesto, cream and parmesan cheese in a bowl. Season with salt and pepper. *(If the mixture is too runny add some more chicken or cheese.)*
- Place four lasagne squares onto a board lined with baking paper. Top each square with a spoonful of pesto chicken mix and spread to the edges. Repeat two more times so each stack has three layers of lasagne and filling.

- Cut one sheet of pastry into quarters and place on a board. You should have enough chicken mixture left to put one last layer on each pastry square. *(Make sure you leave a 1 cm gap around the perimeter.)*
- Place a lasagne stack into the centre of each pastry square. Cut the remaining pastry sheet into quarters and carefully stretch the pastry over the lasagne stacks. Use a fork *(or your fingers)* to seal the edges of the pockets, then brush egg over the top of each.
- Preheat air fryer to 200°C.
- Place pockets into the air fryer and cook at 200°C for 15 minutes or until golden.
- Sprinkle lasagne pockets with extra parmesan and enjoy with roasted cherry tomatoes.

SPICY BACON SCALLOPS

These little suckers are so damn delicious! I cook them for my parents when they stay over so they think I actually know what I'm doing in the kitchen. Works every time!

Makes 20

¼ cup mayonnaise
1 tablespoon sriracha sauce
20 scallops
1 pinch salt
1 pinch pepper
7 rashers streaky bacon, cut into thirds
cooking oil spray

- In a small bowl, mix mayonnaise and sriracha together until combined.
- Preheat air fryer to 200°C.
- Lay scallops out on a plate or chopping board and pat dry with paper towel. Season with salt and pepper.
- Wrap each scallop with a rasher of bacon and secure with a toothpick.
- Spray the air fryer basket with cooking spray. Place the bacon-wrapped scallops into the air fryer in a single layer. *(You may have to cook them in two batches.)*
- Cook at 200°C for 7 minutes. *(Scallops should be non-transparent and bacon should be crispy.)* Cook 1–2 minutes longer if necessary, checking every 60 seconds.
- Place scallops onto a paper towel-lined plate to absorb excess oil then serve with sriracha mayo.

POTATO CHIP-CRUMBED FISH

This takes fish and chips to a whole new dimension.

Makes 4
1 packet (50 g) potato chips (I use Red Rock Deli sea salt and
   balsamic vinegar chips)
1 egg, beaten
4 flathead fillets
cooking oil spray

- Preheat air fryer to 180°C.
- Empty potato chips into a ziplock bag. Remove any excess air and
  close bag. Use a rolling pin to crush potato chips into small crumbs.
  Place crumbs in a medium-sized bowl.
- Add beaten egg to another bowl.
- Dip a fish fillet into the egg mixture and allow the excess to drip off.
  Then dip into the crushed potato chips, completely covering the
  fillet. Repeat with the remaining pieces of fish.
- Spray the air fryer basket with cooking oil spray and place the
  crumbed fish into the air fryer. Spray the fish with more cooking
  oil spray.
- Cook at 180°C for 10–12 minutes or until the fish flakes easily with
  a fork.
- Serve with salad.

BREAKFAST SPRING ROLLS

These breakfast spring rolls are filled with eggs, bacon and veggies. An interesting twist on an egg sandwich. Perfect for making ahead as they are great reheated.

Makes 6

6 eggs
1 tablespoon water
¼ teaspoon salt
¼ teaspoon pepper
3 rashers streaky bacon
2 tablespoons chopped spring onions
2 tablespoons diced capsicum
6 spring roll wrappers
cooking oil spray

- Whisk eggs with water, salt and pepper.
- Dice bacon and add to a medium-sized non-stick frypan. Cook over medium heat for 5 minutes, stirring regularly. Drain off any excess fat and then stir in spring onions and capsicum, cooking for another 2 minutes before setting aside in a bowl. *(You can also cook this step in the air fryer, but I wouldn't try air frying chopped spring onions. They would fly around the air fryer like confetti at a wedding.)*
- Increase temperature to a medium heat and spray frypan with oil. Pour in egg mixture and cook, stirring until eggs are fluffy and cooked through. Stir in bacon mixture and take off the heat.
- Place a spring roll wrapper on a clean, dry surface with corners positioned like a diamond.

- Add ¼ cup of egg mixture on the bottom corner of the wrapper. Carefully lift this corner and wrap it around the filling. Fold the left and right corners in towards the centre and continue to roll into a tight cylinder. Dip your finger into water and run it along the last little flap of the spring roll sheet, then press down softly so the sheet sticks together. Repeat with remaining filling and wrappers.
- Preheat air fryer to 180°C.
- Spray the rolls and the base of the air fryer basket with cooking oil spray.
- Cook the rolls, in batches, at 180°C for 10 minutes, turning halfway, until they are golden and crispy.
- Serve immediately. *(I like to dip mine in salsa.)*

CHEESY CHICKEN NUGGETS

What is better than a chicken nugget? This!

Serves 2
500 g boneless chicken breast
8 Arnott's Country Cheese biscuits
1 cup plain flour
¼ teaspoon salt
¼ teaspoon pepper
2 eggs, beaten
⅓ cup grated parmesan cheese
2 teaspoons dried mixed herbs
cooking oil spray

- On a chopping board, cut chicken into 2.5–3 cm cubes. Set aside.
- Preheat air fryer at 200°C.
- Place the cheese biscuits into a ziplock bag, remove any excess air and secure. Use a rolling pin to crush biscuits into small crumbs.
- Set out three small bowls. In the first bowl, place flour, salt and pepper. Lightly mix. Add beaten eggs to the second bowl and in the third, combine crushed cheese biscuits, parmesan cheese and dried herbs.
- One at a time, coat chicken pieces in the flour, then dip into the egg, then coat with the biscuit mixture. *(You may have to apply some light pressure to help the coating stick to the chicken.)*
- Spray the air fryer basket with cooking oil spray, then place the nuggets into the air fryer in a single layer. *(You may have to cook them in batches.)* Spray the nuggets with cooking oil spray.
- Cook each batch of nuggets at 200°C for approximately 7 minutes, turning halfway, until cooked through and golden.

Dinners are easier when you cook them in the air fryer

Is there anything better than kicking back with a beer, watching your favourite team and eating a few snacks? This weekend, instead of reaching for the potato chips or popcorn, why not try some of these air-fried game-day munchies?

I mean who wouldn't want to put some Chicken Kiev Meatballs into their mouth while they are screaming profanities at the TV?

♫ *Don't forget to make a mess it's all part of the fun* ♫

TANGY PRAWN CAKES

This might just be the recipe that becomes a staple at your home. How can something so simple be so flavourful?

Makes 8–10
400 g prawns, peeled and cooked
1 cup breadcrumbs
2 eggs, beaten
1 tablespoon olive oil
¼ cup chopped spring onions
1 tablespoon chopped fresh dill
1 lemon, juiced and zested
6 cloves garlic, minced
½ teaspoon paprika
½ teaspoon dried parsley
½ teaspoon salt
½ teaspoon pepper

- Dice prawns into 1 cm cubes and add to a large bowl.
- Add breadcrumbs, beaten eggs, olive oil, spring onions, dill, lemon *(juice and zest)*, garlic, paprika, parsley, salt and pepper. Mix gently to combine.
- Preheat air fryer to 190°C.
- Separate the prawn mixture into eight to ten patties. *(You can use your hands or an ice cream scoop if you are scared of getting your hands dirty.)*
- Lay a piece of baking paper inside the air fryer and place half of the prawn cakes on top.
- Cook at 190°C for 8–10 minutes or until you see a nice golden crust. Flip and cook for a further 5 minutes. Repeat with the remaining prawn cakes.
- Serve as finger food or with a side salad.

HAM AND EGG JOEYS

Look, I know everyone thinks their mum is an amazing cook, but seriously, my mum is better than your mum. This one is for her. Thanks, Mum.

Makes 2

1 egg
2 teaspoons milk
2 teaspoons butter
30 g thinly sliced ham
2 tablespoons grated cheese
1 sheet puff pastry, thawed
cooking oil spray

- In a small bowl, gently whisk egg and milk until combined.
- In a small saucepan, heat butter over medium heat. Add egg mixture and stir until eggs are completely cooked through (*make sure there are no watery bits*). Remove from heat and fold in ham and cheese.
- Preheat air fryer to 180°C.
- Cut puff pastry into two rectangles. Scoop half the egg mixture into the centre of each rectangle. Fold the pastry over the filling and pinch the ends to seal.
- Spray the air fryer basket with cooking oil spray and place pastries into the air fryer in a single layer.
- Cook at 180°C for 8–10 minutes or until the pastry is golden brown.

CHICKEN KIEV MEATBALLS

Get ready for a mouth explosion.

Makes 12
½ cup unsalted butter
3 cloves garlic, crushed
1 tablespoon chopped fresh continental parsley
500 g chicken mince
2 eggs, beaten
1 cup panko breadcrumbs
1 teaspoon salt
½ teaspoon pepper
1 teaspoon paprika
cooking oil spray

- In a small bowl, mix butter, garlic and parsley together until evenly combined. On a sheet of baking paper, divide butter mixture into twelve equal parts. Freeze until solid. *(Roughly 20 minutes.)*
- Meanwhile, lay a piece of baking paper onto a board and shape chicken mince into twelve equal golf ball-sized meatballs. Use your finger to make an indent in each meatball.
- Remove frozen butter mixture from freezer and place a piece of butter into the indent of each meatball. Wrap the meat around the butter until it is completely covered, then reshape it into a ball. Repeat with the remaining meatballs and butter.
- Set out two medium-sized bowls. Add beaten egg to one of the bowls and breadcrumbs, salt, pepper and paprika to the other.

- Dip a meatball into the egg then into the breadcrumb mixture. Then dip the crumbed meatball back into the egg and the breadcrumb mixture again. *(This extra coating is to help keep that juicy garlic butter inside the meatball.)* Repeat with remaining meatballs and place on a sheet of baking paper and freeze for 10–15 minutes.
- Preheat air fryer to 200°C.
- Remove meatballs from freezer and place half of the balls into the air fryer. Spray with cooking oil spray.
- Cook at 200°C for 5 minutes. Turn, spray again with cooking oil and cook for a further 5 minutes. Repeat with the remaining meatballs.

BOOF'S SAUSAGE AND GRUEL ROLLS

Every time my dad cooks a BBQ, he makes this amazing caramelised onion concoction that he calls 'gruel'. This is my take on his famous recipe.

Makes 8–10
½ tablespoon olive oil
1 large onion, sliced
4 cloves garlic, chopped
2 tomatoes, diced
1 tablespoon brown sugar
8 thin beef sausages
½ tablespoon oregano
½ teaspoon salt
½ teaspoon pepper
2 sheets puff pastry, thawed
1 egg, beaten

- Heat a saucepan over medium–high heat. Heat olive oil, then add sliced onion and cook, stirring occasionally, for 3 minutes, until the onion starts to soften. Add chopped garlic, diced tomatoes and brown sugar. Reduce heat to medium and cook for 5 minutes or until the tomato and onion are soft and cooked through. Remove from heat, pour into a small bowl and whack it in the fridge to cool down. *(This is the gruel.)*
- Preheat air fryer to 200°C.

- Remove the casing from the sausages and place the meat into a medium-sized bowl. Add oregano, salt and pepper and mix to combine.
- Lay a sheet puff pastry onto a dry surface. Place half the sausage meat onto the bottom part of the pastry and make a sausage shape the same width as the pastry. Press down firmly with your hand to slightly flatten it out. Scoop out half the gruel and evenly distribute it over the top of the sausage meat. Roll the pastry over the meat and gruel, then roll again. Cut off excess pastry and repeat with the remaining pastry, sausage and gruel.
- Cut sausage rolls into the desired size (*I like to cut them into quarters*). Brush beaten egg over the tops and sides of each piece.
- Add sausage rolls, in a single layer, to the air fryer and cook at 200°C for 10–12 minutes or until pastry is golden and sausage is cooked.
- Serve as they are or with tomato sauce.

The best thing about trying something new is that it's really really fun

CRUNCHY POTATO SKINS

You will never throw away your potato peels again.

Serves 2–4
4 large washed potatoes
1 tablespoon olive oil
1 teaspoon paprika
salt and pepper

- Rinse and wash the potatoes thoroughly.
- Using a potato peeler, peel the potatoes. Try to make the peels as big as possible *(you will have some smaller ones but that is fine, the smaller they are, the crispier they become).* Set the potatoes aside for later use. *(We only need the peels for this recipe.)*
- Add the peels to a large bowl. Add olive oil, paprika, salt and pepper then toss to combine.
- Preheat air fryer to 200°C.
- Add the seasoned potato skins to the air fryer and cook at 200°C for 10–15 minutes *(tossing regularly, every 2–3 minutes)* or until the skins are golden and crispy.
- Remove potato skins from the air fryer. Add a touch more salt and serve with ketchup or any sauce you like.
- Enjoy!

CHICKEN AND CORN BASEBALLS

When I was a kid, I used to get something similar to these from our local chicken shop. It's funny how strong the connection between food and memory can be.

Makes 6

2 cups mashed potato
1 cup shredded chicken
½ cup grated cheese
¼ cup corn kernels
½ teaspoon salt
½ teaspoon pepper
¼ teaspoon paprika
1 cup plain flour
2 eggs, beaten
1 cup panko breadcrumbs
cooking oil spray

- In a large bowl, add mashed potato, shredded chicken, cheese, corn, salt, pepper and paprika. Mix to combine. *(It's easier if you just use your hands, plus it's fun to get a bit messy in the kitchen.)*
- Separate potato mixture into six equal parts. Shape each part into a ball and set down onto a sheet of baking paper.
- Preheat the air fryer to 180°C.
- Set out three medium-sized bowls. Add flour to the first bowl, beaten egg to the second and breadcrumbs to the third.
- Dip a potato ball into the flour and cover. Shake off any excess flour then dip into the egg and cover completely. Finally, dip the ball into the breadcrumbs, making sure that the entire ball is crumbed. Set aside and repeat with remaining balls.
- Spray the base of the air fryer basket with cooking oil spray, then place the balls into the air fryer in a single layer. Spray the balls with some more cooking oil spray.
- Cook at 180°C for 10 minutes, turning halfway, until golden and crispy.

MINI CHEESE AND SPINACH CALZONES

These little snacks should be the perfect appetisers. The problem is, you can't stop eating them, so you end up losing your appetite!

Makes 10–12
1 fresh pizza dough ball (you can make your own dough if you like, but I find the lazy way is just as delicious)
1 tablespoon olive oil
1 small brown onion, finely diced
2 cloves garlic, minced
120 g baby spinach
1 cup ricotta
salt and pepper to taste
½ cup fetta, crumbled
handful plain flour (for rolling out the dough)

- Remove pizza dough from fridge. Let rest for 1 hour or until it reaches room temperature.
- Heat olive oil in a non-stick saucepan over medium heat, then add onion and garlic. Cook for a few minutes or until the onion softens. Add spinach and stir until spinach is wilted and combined with the onion, roughly 2 minutes. Take off heat and set aside. *(You can also use frozen spinach for this recipe, it just takes a bit longer to thaw and cook. Laziness is a virtue.)*
- In a large bowl, add ricotta and a generous amount of salt and pepper. Mix to combine. Then add the spinach mix and fetta and mix until all ingredients are combined.

- On a lightly floured surface, roll out the pizza dough until ½ cm thick. Use a cookie cutter *(I just use a large drinking glass)* to cut out eight to ten rounds of dough. Move the rounds onto a baking paper-lined baking sheet. Gather up the dough scraps, re-roll and repeat cutting until you have used up all the dough.
- Top each round with a generous spoonful of the spinach mixture, making sure to leave some room around the edges.
- One at a time, fold each dough round in half, then pinch the edges together to seal. *(If the dough doesn't stick together, use your finger to run some water around the edges.)* Once each calzone is sealed, use a fork to crimp the edges to further seal.
- Preheat air fryer to 190°C.
- Working in batches of four at a time, cook the calzones in the air fryer at 190°C for 8 minutes or until golden brown and crisp.

I had a huge appetite when I was a kid. I think it was because I was growing about an inch per week. I stopped growing at around seventeen years old, reaching a towering six feet and three inches! Imagine trying to feed a kid of that size.

Luckily, my mum was prepared. She would always have plenty of food ready for me when I got home from school, which made me feel loved ... and full!

This chapter is all about creating delicious snacks for those hungry kids. Recipes such as Sweet Potato Gems, Ham and Cheese Spinach Puffs, or my favourite, Deconstructed Caramello S'Mores will curb that hunger.

♫ Then cover it in crumbs, ooh ♫
yum yum yum ♪

DECONSTRUCTED CARAMELLO S'MORES

Since creating this recipe, any time anyone in my family has a birthday, they request these. We even put birthday candles in them! There is something about the taste and texture that makes you feel like they are only to be eaten on special occasions. Kind of like dessert caviar!

Makes 6

6 large (35 g) Caramello Koalas
3 digestive biscuits
2 sheets puff pastry, partially thawed
12 white marshmallows
1 tablespoon icing sugar

- Before preparing, freeze the Caramello Koalas in their wrappers for 1 hour.
- Preheat air fryer to 200°C.
- In a small bowl, crush the digestive biscuits with your fingers.
- Place a sheet of pastry onto a large board. Cut in half crossways, then into three lengthways (*you should end up with six rectangles, 8 x 12 cm.*) Sprinkle about 2 teaspoons biscuit crumbs into the centre of three pastry rectangles. Top with a Caramello Koala then cover with remaining pastry pieces. Seal the edges. Repeat with remaining pastry to make six s'mores in total.
- Place s'mores into the air fryer on a piece of baking paper and air fry at 200°C for about 10–12 minutes or until lightly browned (*not too dark as there is more cooking to be done*).

Sizzler Copycat Toast
page 178

Chicken-Twisties Chicken
page 199

Leftover Mac and Cheese
Sausages page 50

Big Mac Spring Rolls
Page 72

Cheeseburger Onion Rings Page 24

Wagon Wheel
Pies
page 35

Caramilk Poppers
page 30

- Remove s'mores from air fryer and top each with two marshmallows. Return to the air fryer and cook at 200°C for 3–5 minutes or until the marshmallows are gooey. *(Be sure to keep an eye on the s'mores as the marshmallows like to fly around the air fryer and can melt very quickly.)*
- Remove s'mores from air fryer and dust with icing sugar, then sprinkle with remaining biscuit crumbs. Wait a few minutes before serving *(I like mine with ice cream)* as the caramel and marshmallow are hot straight from the air fryer.

♫ *I just air fried some biscuits and darn it felt so good* ♫

TIM CROWN BROWNIES

Sweet, gooey on the inside, with a crispy exterior. Did I just describe myself?

Makes 6–10
1 packet Tim Tams
1 packet Caramel Crowns
1 packet brownie mix
2 eggs
12 g unsalted butter, melted

- Preheat air fryer to 160°C.
- Crush Tim Tams and ½ packet of Caramel Crowns into a large mixing bowl. Add ¾ brownie mix, eggs and butter. Stir until gooey and combined.
- Add mixture to a lined baking tray. *(I use a silicone tray but you can use any oven-proof tray that will fit inside your air fryer. You can even make individual brownies if you only have patty pans.)*
- Arrange the remaining Caramel Crowns on top.
- Place brownie into air fryer and cook at 160°C for 25–30 minutes. When the brownie is finished cooking, poke a skewer or a knife into the centre. You should see gooey crumbs on the skewer. If not, cook for another 5–10 minutes. *(The thinner the brownie, the quicker it cooks.)*
- Rest for 20 minutes in the baking tray then remove brownie from the tray and rest on a wire rack for a further 10–15 minutes.
- Cut into pieces and serve with ice cream if desired.
  (I sometimes make a brownie ice cream sandwich.)

HAM AND CHEESE SPINACH PUFFS

This is a great one for the kids. Super fun and easy to make.

Makes 4
2 sheets puff pastry, thawed
30 g baby spinach
8 slices deli ham
4 slices Swiss cheese
1 egg, beaten

- Cut pastry sheets in half, making four rectangles.
- On each pastry rectangle, add a single layer of spinach leaves, leaving a 2 cm space around the edges of the pastry. Place two slices of ham on top of the spinach, then a slice of cheese, right in the centre.
- Fold the top and bottom edges of the pastry over the filling, then fold both left and right sides. *(You should be left with a hole in the top of the pastry where you can see a window of cheese.)* Pinch the edges of the pastry to secure. Repeat with remaining pastries, then brush with egg.
- Preheat air fryer to 180°C.
- Cook pastries in batches at 180°C for 8–10 minutes, until pastry is golden and cheese is melted and oozing.

SWEET POTATO GEMS (WITH SPICY MAYO)

Americans call them tots, but Aussies call them gems. Why? It doesn't matter because they taste great either way.

Serves 2–4

Spicy Mayo

½ cup mayonnaise
1 tablespoon sriracha
1 teaspoon lemon juice
pepper to taste

Potato Gems

1 kg sweet potatoes
½ teaspoon onion powder
½ teaspoon garlic powder
1 teaspoon salt
½ teaspoon pepper
cooking oil spray

- In a small bowl, combine mayonnaise, sriracha, lemon juice and pepper. Cover and set aside in the fridge.
- Peel the sweet potatoes then add to a medium-sized saucepan. Cover the potatoes with water and bring to a boil over high heat. Once boiling, cover the saucepan and reduce heat to medium. Boil for 8 minutes or until the potatoes are half cooked. (*A great way to check is piercing the potatoes with a fork. The fork should easily pierce the potato but it should still be firm.*) Drain the potatoes and let them cool until they are easy to handle (*about 15 minutes*).
- Grate the potatoes with the larges holes of a box grater into a large bowl.

- Add onion powder, garlic powder, salt and pepper. Mix gently to combine.
- Lay some baking paper onto a board. Scoop out 1 tablespoon of potato mixture and shape it into a gem/tot. Place onto the baking paper and repeat with the remaining potato mixture. *(If the potato is a bit sticky and hard to handle, moisten your hands with a bit of water.)* Once created, let the potato gems air dry for 5 minutes.
- Preheat the air fryer to 180°C.
- Spray the air fryer basket with cooking oil spray. Add half the potato gems to the air fryer in a single layer, making sure they aren't touching one another.
- Spray the potato gems with some more cooking oil spray then cook at 180°C for 15 minutes. Shake the basket every 5 minutes so they cook evenly and they don't stick to the air fryer.
- Repeat with the remaining potato gems. *(If you want to keep the first batch warm, you can put them in the oven at 150°C while you wait for the second batch to cook.)*
- Serve warm with spicy mayo dipping sauce.

CHICKEN PIZZA ROLLS

I make these bad boys at least once a week. I just love how cheesy and easy they are!

Makes 2

1 chicken breast
2 tablespoons pizza sauce
8 slices pepperoni
4 slices Swiss cheese
½ cup plain flour
½ teaspoon salt
½ teaspoon pepper
1 egg, beaten
1 cup panko breadcrumbs

- Preheat air fryer to 180°C.
- Place chicken onto a chopping board and cut in half, running your knife parallel to the board to make two thin, flat pieces. *(I like to place my hand flat on top of the chicken as I'm cutting it because it's easier to make a straighter cut.)* Cover the chicken with cling wrap and use a meat tenderiser *(I like to call it the squishy hammer)* to flatten out evenly to about 1 cm thick.
- Remove cling wrap *(a very important step, LOL)*.
- Spread 1 tablespoon pizza sauce evenly over one chicken piece, then top with four slices pepperoni and two slices cheese. Starting at one end, roll up the chicken and secure with a toothpick. Repeat with second piece of chicken.

- Set out three medium-sized bowls. Add flour, salt and pepper to the first bowl, beaten egg to the second and breadcrumbs to the third.
- Dip both chicken pizza rolls, one by one, into the flour, then egg, then breadcrumbs. Make sure to seal the open sides of the rolls by completely covering in each.
- Place into air fryer and cook at 180°C for 8–10 minutes or until golden and the chicken is fully cooked.
- Serve with your choice of side.

CRUNCHY MEXICAN QUESADILLA

This is my (Mexican) take on the classic Australian chip sandwich.

Makes 1
½ cup shredded chicken
½ tablespoon taco seasoning
¼ cup shredded cheese
2 large flour tortillas
large handful corn chips
1 tomato, diced
½ cup shredded lettuce
¼ cup sour cream
cooking oil spray

- Preheat air fryer to 200°C.
- In a large bowl, combine shredded chicken, taco seasoning and shredded cheese.
- Remove air fryer basket and place a tortilla inside. Spoon chicken mixture onto the tortilla and spread evenly, covering completely. Top with corn chips, tomato and lettuce.
- Spread the sour cream evenly over the second tortilla then place it, sour cream side down, onto the other tortilla. Secure with a couple of toothpicks.
- Spray the tortilla with cooking oil spray then place the basket back into the air fryer. Cook at 200°C for 3–5 minutes, until golden. Flip, then spray with more cooking oil spray. Cook for a further 3–5 minutes, until golden and cheese is oozing.
- Cut in half and serve hot.

♫ Then put it in the air fryer ♪
at 200 degrees
celsius of course
♪ ♪ for about six minutes. please! ♫

IMPRESS YOUR PARTNER

There is something special about cooking food for your partner. Whether after a hard day at work or Sunday breakfast, it's a beautiful thing to feed and be fed. But every now and then your partner makes you something so delicious that the food goes straight down your throat and into your heart. You can taste the effort!

♫ *Gnocchi for lunch, gnocchi for tea, gnocchi in the air fryer for me!* ♫

VEGETARIAN STUFFED CAPSICUMS

I don't create many vegetarian recipes, but this one is crazy good.

Makes 2
2 medium red capsicums
125 g cooked brown rice
½ red onion, diced
2 tablespoons chopped fresh basil
1 tomato, diced
¼ cup grated cheese
salt and pepper to taste

- Preheat air fryer to 180°C.
- Cut the tops off the capsicums. Remove seeds and set aside.
- Dice the cut-off pieces into small cubes and add to a large bowl.
- Add brown rice, onion, basil, tomato, cheese, salt and pepper and mix well.
- Fill both capsicums with the rice mixture.
- Cook at 180°C for 10–15 minutes or until slightly charred and cooked through.

GRIGGSY'S PORK BELLY

The crackling on this pork belly just might save your life.

Serves 2–3
1 kg pork belly
1 tablespoon olive oil
1 tablespoon flaky salt

- Pat the pork belly dry with paper towel. It's important to remove as much moisture as possible.
- Use a small sharp knife to deeply score the rind at 1 cm intervals. *(Be careful not to cut into the meat as it will release moisture during cooking and ruin the crackling.)* Place the pork belly uncovered in the fridge for 1–24 hours *(depending on the amount of time you have)*. This will dry out the rind and make a better crackling.
- When you are ready to cook, place the pork, skin side up, onto a wire rack over the sink. Poor a jug of boiling water over the rind, then pat dry thoroughly with paper towel.
- Rub the entire roast with oil and salt, making sure the oil and salt penetrates the scoring in the rind.
- Preheat the air fryer to 200°C.
- Place the pork into the air fryer, rind-side up. Set timer for 25 minutes and cook at 200°C until the rind crackles. Reduce temperature to 160°C and cook for a further 30 minutes, until pork is tender and cooked through.
- Rest for 10–15 minutes before carving and serving with your favourite sides.

MAC AND CHEESE-STUFFED CHICKEN

I would bathe in a tub of mac and cheese if it was socially acceptable.

Makes 2
150 g elbow macaroni
2 tablespoons butter
2 tablespoons plain flour
½ teaspoon salt
pepper to taste
1 cup milk
1 cup grated cheese
2 chicken breasts
½ tablespoon paprika

- Bring a large pot of water to a boil. Cook macaroni for 8 minutes, stirring occasionally, until cooked through but still firm to the bite. Drain and set aside.
- Melt butter in a saucepan over medium heat. Stir in flour, salt and pepper until smooth. Slowly pour milk into the pan while continuously stirring, until mixture is smooth and bubbling. Add cheese and stir until melted.
- Remove from heat and add cooked macaroni. Stir until fully combined. Set aside.
- Preheat air fryer to 180°C.
- Using a sharp knife, pierce the wide end of the chicken breast, making a large cavity. Be careful not to cut all the way through the chicken. Use your fingers to widen the hole so that you can fit a good amount of mac and cheese inside. Repeat with the remaining chicken breast.

- Scoop out some mac and cheese and carefully push it into the cavity of the chicken. Press down firmly and keep adding until the cavity is almost full. Repeat with the second chicken breast and remaining mac and cheese. Use a couple of toothpicks to seal the cavity. Sprinkle both sides of the chicken with paprika and a pinch of salt and pepper.
- Place chicken into air fryer and cook at 180°C for 18–20 minutes, turning halfway. (*Keep an eye on your chicken while it is cooking. Times can differ dramatically depending on the size of the chicken breasts.*)
- Serve with vegetables or a salad.

♪ *Sometimes I just wanna be alone with Mac 'n' cheese* ♫

SPANAKOPITA BITES

You will be in the good books for weeks after your partner tries these.

Makes 8
75 g butter, melted
8 sheets filo pastry
250 g frozen chopped spinach, thawed
4 eggs
½ cup fetta cheese, crumbled, plus extra for serving
salt and pepper to taste

- Preheat air fryer to 160°C.
- Brush the holes of a muffin tin with ⅓ cup butter. *(Make sure you have a muffin tin that fits into your air fryer, or use individual silicone cups.)*
- Brush a sheet of pastry with butter, fold over and brush again. Fold again and cut into two squares. Brush with butter and stack at a 90° angle. Repeat with remaining sheets and butter, then add the pastry stacks to the muffin tins, creating a case.
- Drain spinach and squeeze out excess moisture.
- In a large bowl, whisk eggs, then add spinach and fetta. Add a pinch of salt and pepper and mix to combine. Divide mixture between muffin tins then gently fold the edges of the filo pastry over the filling to partially cover. Brush the tops of the pastry with remaining butter.
- Place muffin tin into the air fryer and cook at 160°C for 20–25 minutes or until pastry is golden and the filling is cooked through.
- Rest for 5 minutes then serve with a sprinkle of fetta.

♫ *I wanna wrap myself in pastry because I think I'd be a really nice pie* ♫

WEEKNIGHT DINNERS

If you're like me, you are more than happy to spend a lot of money on a good meal but also like to cook weekly dinners without breaking the bank. Just because something is affordable doesn't mean it has to taste bad. Come with me on a frugal journey that will put good food in your mouth and leave money in your pocket.

Recipes such as Kasey's Sausage Surprise, Deluxe Chicken Thighs and Moe's Poached Paprika Chicken are perfect for those of you who want great food at a great price.

♫ *I wanna take that forbidden fruit and put it in my mouth* ♪

KASEY'S SAUSAGE SURPRISE

Who doesn't love a surprise sausage?

Serves 2–3

8 thin beef sausages
1 cup diced red potatoes
1 cup green beans, halved
1 head broccoli, broken into small florets
1 red capsicum, chopped
6 tablespoons olive oil
¼ teaspoon chilli flakes
1 teaspoon paprika
½ teaspoon garlic powder
1 teaspoon dried thyme
1 tablespoon dried oregano
1 tablespoon dried parsley
1 tablespoon dried basil
salt and pepper to taste

- Preheat air fryer to 200°C.
- Cut sausages into 2 cm thick pieces and add to a large mixing bowl.
- Add potatoes, beans, broccoli, capsicum and olive oil, then mix to combine. Finally, add the remaining ingredients and toss well until fully combined.
- Pour the sausage and vegetable mix directly into the air fryer basket.
- Cook at 200°C for 15–20 minutes, shaking the basket every 3–4 minutes. Remove from air fryer when the sausages are cooked through and the vegetables are tender.

MOE'S POACHED PAPRIKA CHICKEN

This is a biweekly staple in our house. It's healthy, filling, and delicious.

Makes 2

2 chicken breasts
2 tablespoons olive oil
1 tablespoon paprika
1 tablespoon salt
1 tablespoon pepper
4 cloves garlic, peeled

- Preheat air fryer to 200°C.
- On a dry surface, lay out two pieces of aluminium foil about 30 cm x 30 cm.
- Place a chicken breast on each piece of foil. Drizzle with half the olive oil, then sprinkle on half the paprika, salt and pepper. Flip the chicken breasts over and drizzle with remaining olive oil and sprinkle with remaining paprika, salt and pepper. Then place two cloves of garlic underneath each piece of chicken.
- Fold the foil over the chicken then fold in the sides of the foil, making a sealed steam pouch.
- Place pouches into the air fryer and cook at 200°C for 20 minutes or until the chicken is fully cooked. (*A great way to test if the chicken is cooked is to check the juices. If the juice runs clear it is cooked, but if it isn't, cook for a further 3–5 minutes.*)
- Serve with baked vegetables or salad.

DELUXE CHICKEN THIGHS

Chicken and air frying are probably the ultimate duo. But if you are bored of the same old crumbed chicken, this recipe will spice things up.

Makes 4

1 teaspoon salt
¼ teaspoon pepper
2 teaspoons garlic powder
¼ teaspoon ground coriander seeds
¼ teaspoon turmeric
2 teaspoons paprika
¼ teaspoon ground ginger
4 chicken thighs, bone in and skin on

- Preheat air fryer to 200°C.
- In a small bowl, mix salt, pepper, garlic powder, coriander, turmeric, paprika and ginger.
- Rub the spice mixture directly all over each chicken thigh.
- Place the chicken thighs into the air fryer, skin side up and cook at 200°C for 10 minutes. Turn the chicken thighs over and cook for a further 5 minutes or until the chicken is cooked though. (*I suggest using a meat thermometer to check the chicken. When cooked, the internal temperature must reach 75°C.*)
- Serve with mashed potato and vegetables.

NACHOS-FILLED BAKED POTATOES

Air fried potatoes are so much better than oven baked because they get this amazing crispy exterior. So why not lift your potato game further with a bit of nachos?

Makes 4

4 medium washed potatoes
cooking oil spray
½ teaspoon salt
½ teaspoon garlic powder
handful corn chips
¼ cup black beans
¼ cup grated cheese
1 tomato, diced
¼ cup sour cream

- Preheat air fryer to 200°C.
- Place potatoes into the air fryer basket and spray with cooking oil spray. Sprinkle all sides with salt and garlic powder. Use your hands to rub the salt and oil onto the potatoes so that they are evenly coated.
- Cook at 200°C for 40 minutes, rotating after 20 minutes.
- Remove from air fryer and cut a slit through the middle of the potatoes, making sure not to cut all the way through the potato. Add some corn chips into the potatoes, then top with beans and cheese.
- Place the potatoes back into the air fryer for 3–5 minutes or until the cheese is melted and the corn chips are slightly charred.
- Serve with diced tomato and a dollop of sour cream.

CORN CHIPS AND SALSA CHICKEN

Sometimes when you are experimenting in the kitchen, you create something that is surprisingly delicious. This recipe was intended to be a bit of a joke, but it ended up tasting amazing.

Makes 2

1 large chicken breast
large handful corn chips
½ cup salsa
½ cup plain flour
cooking oil spray

- Cut the chicken breast in half by running a knife parallel with the chopping board, so you end up with two identical thinner pieces of chicken.
- Add corn chips to a ziplock bag and seal it, removing any excess air. Use a rolling pin to crush the corn chips into small crumbs then pour into a medium-sized bowl. Add salsa to a second bowl and flour to a third.
- Dip a piece of chicken into the flour, covering completely. Shake off any excess then dip into the salsa. Once covered, dip the chicken into the corn chip crumbs and thoroughly coat. Repeat with the remaining piece of chicken.
- Preheat air fryer to 200°C.
- Spray the base of the air fryer basket with cooking oil, then place the crumbed chicken inside before spraying the chicken with a little more oil.
- Cook at 200°C for 10 minutes, turning halfway, until golden and the chicken is fully cooked.

Just put these things in the air fryer
and out comes a beautiful dinner

SIMPLE SIDES

Side dishes are a great way to enhance a meal. But I have to admit, I don't tend to put much effort into sides because I'm lazy. If you are also lazy or you just want some simple side dishes to spruce up a meal, these recipes are for you.

This delicious treat will turn your frown upside down

SPICY PANKO CARROTS

I always seem to have a bag of carrots hanging around the kitchen. This recipe is great when you want to use up some forgotten carrots because they'll taste less like carrots and more like chicken wings! This is one of my favourite sides. I'm usually singing this while I'm making them: 'Carrots are cool, carrots are cool, but crumbed carrots are cooler.'

Serves 2

8 small carrots
cooking oil spray
½ teaspoon salt
½ teaspoon pepper
½ cup mayonnaise
¼ cup hot sauce (I like to use Truff hot sauce but any will do)
½ cup plain flour
1 cup panko breadcrumbs

- Preheat air fryer to 200°C.
- Trim the tops off the carrots and peel them, then place into a bowl. Spray with some cooking oil and sprinkle with salt and pepper before giving them a good shake to ensure all carrots are evenly coated.
- Air fry at 200°C for 5–10 minutes or until almost cooked. (*I like to use a toothpick to press into the carrots. If the toothpick slides through the carrot with ease, it's ready.*)

- Meanwhile, in a medium-sized bowl, mix the mayonnaise and hot sauce together until combined. Reserve ¼ of the mixture for later.
- Add flour to another bowl and breadcrumbs to a third.
- Take the carrots out of the air fryer and let them cool until they don't burn your hand when touched. *(You can put them into the fridge to speed up the process.)*
- Once carrots are cooled, one by one, cover with flour, then spicy mayonnaise, then breadcrumbs.
- Place carrots back into the air fryer and cook at 200°C for about 5 minutes or until golden brown. *(For less mess, you can place the carrots onto a piece of baking paper inside the air fryer.)*
- Serve with the remaining spicy mayonnaise mixture as a dip.

♫ *Carrots are cool, but crumbed carrots are cooler* ♪

GARLIC ROSEMARY BRUSSELS SPROUTS

I don't know why brussels sprouts get such a bad reputation. Try these and they might just change your mind.

Serves 2

3 tablespoons olive oil
4 garlic cloves, minced
½ teaspoon salt
½ teaspoon pepper
500 g brussels sprouts, trimmed and halved
½ cup panko breadcrumbs
2 teaspoons fresh rosemary, finely chopped

- Preheat air fryer to 180°C.
- In a small microwave-safe bowl, add oil, garlic, salt and pepper and microwave on high for 30 seconds.
- Add brussels sprouts to a large bowl and toss with 2 tablespoons of olive oil mixture.
- Add the seasoned brussels sprouts to the air fryer and cook for 5 minutes at 180°C. Stir the sprouts then cook for a further 3 minutes, stir again, and cook for another 3–5 minutes or until lightly browned and almost tender.
- In a small bowl, combine breadcrumbs, rosemary and remaining oil mixture. Sprinkle over the sprouts then continue cooking for a further 4 minutes or until the breadcrumbs are browned and sprouts are tender.
- Serve with your choice of protein.

SWEET CRUMBED ASPARAGUS

Pair this with a juicy steak or a nice piece of salmon.

Serves 2

2 bunches asparagus
50 g pistachio nuts
1 tablespoon olive oil
1 tablespoon honey
pinch salt

- Preheat air fryer to 200°C.
- Prepare asparagus by snapping off the woody parts at the base of the stem. Place them into a medium-sized bowl.
- Chop pistachios into small pieces and add to the bowl, then add the olive oil and mix to coat.
- Add the asparagus to the air fryer and cook at 200°C for 10 minutes. Give them a toss halfway through.
- Drizzle asparagus with honey and sprinkle with salt then serve.

AUNTY MARGIE'S ULTIMATE GARLIC BREAD

Vampires beware!

Makes 2

2 large white bread rolls
⅓ cup salted butter, softened
6 garlic cloves, minced
1 teaspoon Italian seasoning
¼ cup grated parmesan cheese

- Preheat air fryer to 200°C.
- Using a bread knife, make about five incisions into the top of each bread roll, making sure not to cut all the way through. (*You are basically making little pockets for the garlic butter.*)
- In a small bowl, add softened butter, minced garlic, Italian seasoning and parmesan cheese. Stir to combine.
- Spread the garlic butter evenly over the bread rolls, making sure to get the butter inside the incisions. (*You really want to get as much butter as you can inside the bread roll, whilst still having enough butter to cover the entire roll.*)
- Place the rolls into the air fryer and cook at 200°C for 10 minutes or until the butter is melted and bubbly and the roll is crispy.

♫ *Squish the carbs onto the carbs* ♪
then add another carb ♫

DANGEROUS DESSERTS

My favourite movie growing up was *Willy Wonka & the Chocolate Factory.* I was completely in awe of the marvellous candy creations and slightly scared of the Oompa Loompas. I'm not saying that the desserts in this chapter will make you fly or turn you into a blueberry but consider this your golden ticket to a few of my favourite sweeties.

Be enchanted by my Nutella and Strawberry Wontons, taste the mystically delicious Chocolate Croissant Pudding or conjure up the Easiest Peanut Butter Cookies. These sweets will definitely get Grandpa Joe out of bed!

And now you're really
cooking. baaaaby

EASIEST PEANUT BUTTER COOKIES

You could almost make these with your eyes closed.

Makes 12
1 cup smooth natural peanut butter
2 tablespoons maple syrup

- Preheat air fryer to 180°C.
- In a medium-sized bowl, mix peanut butter *(has to be natural with no added sugar)* and maple syrup until fully combined. Then keep mixing until the batter thickens. *(The batter won't feel like regular cookie dough but it should become firm enough to shape with your hands.)*
- Line the air fryer basket with some baking paper.
- Scoop up roughly 1½ tablespoons of dough and place it onto the baking sheet in the air fryer. Repeat with remaining dough, making sure to space the cookies about 5 cm apart. *(You may have to do them in batches, depending on the size of your air fryer.)* Gently flatten each ball of dough into a round disc. And if you are feeling artistic, you can make a little pattern on the top of the cookies with a fork or a toothpick.
- Air fry the cookies at 180°C for 7–10 minutes or until the surface of the cookies becomes dry.
- Let cookies cool on a piece of baking paper until they are set.

NUTELLA AND STRAWBERRY WONTONS

When making desserts, strawberries are your friend. Nutella is your mistress.

Makes 14

14 wonton wrappers
½ cup Nutella
½ cup diced strawberries
cooking oil spray
1 tablespoon icing sugar

- Place a sheet of baking paper onto a board. Lay out the wonton wrappers, four at a time.
- Spoon a teaspoon of Nutella into the centre of each wonton wrapper, then a teaspoon of diced strawberries.
- Wet your finger and run it over the outside edges of the wonton wrappers. Fold over the wrapper corner to corner to make a triangle and pinch the sides together to seal. Repeat with the remaining wontons.
- Preheat air fryer to 180°C.
- Spray air fryer basket with cooking oil spray and place wontons inside in a single layer. Spray the wontons with a little bit more cooking oil spray. *(You will have to cook the wontons in batches.)*
- Cook at 180°C for 8 minutes, turning halfway, until golden and crisp.
- Dust with icing sugar and serve.

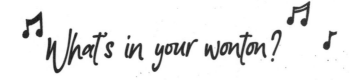

What's in your wonton?

NUTELLA HONEYCOMB HAND PIES

Hand pies are great because they are so much easier to make than regular pies.

Makes 6
2 sheets shortcrust pastry, thawed
2 large Cadbury Crunchies
6 tablespoons Nutella
1 cup icing sugar
2 tablespoons milk

- On a dry surface, cut 10 cm circles out of the shortcrust pastry. You should get three circles per sheet. *(If you don't have a cookie cutter that size, use a small bowl and cut around the edge.)*
- Remove Crunchies from wrapper and place into a ziplock bag. Seal the bag, making sure to release any excess air. Use a rolling pin or a meat tenderiser to crush the Crunchies into crumbs. Place into a small bowl.
- Add a tablespoon of Nutella to the centre of each pastry circle. Then add a tablespoon of crushed Crunchie on top of the Nutella. Make sure to save one tablespoon of crumbs for later.
- Moisten the edges of the circle with a little bit of water, then fold over to make a semicircle. Press down on the edges to seal in the filling *(don't worry if some comes out)*. Then crimp the edges with a fork and poke a couple of holes into the top of the pie with a toothpick.
- Preheat air fryer to 190°C.

- Line the air fryer basket with baking paper and place three pies into the air fryer. Cook at 190°C for 7–9 minutes or until pies are golden brown. Repeat with remaining pies.
- Meanwhile, in a large bowl, whisk the icing sugar and milk together until it becomes a smooth glaze.
- Dip each pie into the glaze and set aside on a sheet of baking paper. Make sure to completely cover the entire pie with glaze then sprinkle pies with the remaining Crunchie crumbs. Let the pies cool and set for at least 15 minutes, then serve.

I wanna be a pie

APPLE FRITTERS

I'm not sure which part of this recipe I like the most: the fritters or the glaze.

Makes 6–8
Fritters
cooking oil spray
1 cup plain flour
5½ tablespoons white sugar
¼ cup milk
1 egg
1 teaspoon baking powder
1 pinch salt
¼ teaspoon cinnamon
1 apple, peeled, cored and diced

Glaze
½ cup icing sugar
¾ tablespoon milk
¼ teaspoon vanilla extract
¼ teaspoon cinnamon

- Preheat air fryer to 180°C. Cut out a round piece of baking paper and place into the bottom of the air fryer. Spray with cooking oil spray. (*An easy way to measure the baking paper is to place your air fryer basket on top of a sheet of baking paper and cut around the edge.*)
- In a small bowl, mix the flour, ¼ cup sugar, milk, egg, baking powder and salt until combined.

- In another bowl, mix remaining sugar with cinnamon then sprinkle over apple and toss until coated. Then pour batter over the apples and mix until combined.
- Use a cooking scoop or spoon to drop golf ball-sized fritters onto the baking paper inside the air fryer basket.
- Cook for 5 minutes then flip fritters and cook for another 5 minutes or until golden.
- Meanwhile, make the glaze by mixing icing sugar, milk, vanilla extract *(you can also use caramel flavouring)* and cinnamon in a bowl.
- Transfer fritters to a cooling rack and allow to cool for 5 minutes before drizzling with the glaze. Let the glaze set for another 5 minutes before serving.

CHOCOLATE CROISSANT PUDDING

I've always loved the word pudding ... say it ... pudding. Now I'm hungry.

Serves 4–6
2 croissants
½ cup chocolate chips
½ cup milk
2 tablespoons sugar
2 eggs
1½ tablespoons cocoa powder
¼ teaspoon vanilla extract
1 teaspoon icing sugar

- Line a 15 cm round baking dish with baking paper.
- Cut croissants into 2.5 cm cubes. *(If you don't have croissants you can use brioche bread or even white bread, but it won't be as tasty.)*
- Add half of the chopped croissant to the baking dish in a single layer and sprinkle chocolate chips evenly over. Add the remaining croissant pieces on top in another layer.
- In a large bowl, add milk, sugar, eggs, cocoa powder and vanilla extract. Whisk together to combine, making a smooth chocolate custard-like mixture. Pour the chocolate mixture over the croissants and use a fork to push them down so they are completely covered by the custard.

- Let the pudding rest for 15 minutes so the croissants can soak up the custard. *(Make sure you don't skip this step because you really need the croissants to soak up all that gooey goodness.)*
- Preheat air fryer to 170°C.
- Place the baking dish into the air fryer and cook at 170°C for 15 minutes. Check to see if it's cooked by poking a knife into the middle of the pudding. If the knife comes out sticky, cook for another 5 minutes.
- Let the pudding rest for 10–15 minutes then sprinkle with icing sugar and serve with a scoop of ice cream.

If you like chocolate, wow that's great. If you don't like chocolate, you're not my mate.

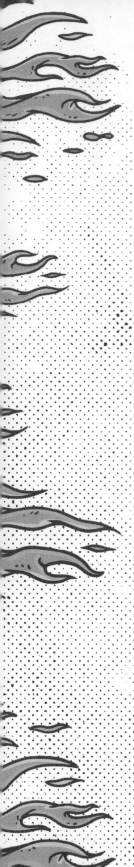

SNACK ATTACK

It's 10 pm. You are about to watch the final episode of some obscure TV show that you should've stopped watching after the first episode. You hear a deep rumble. It's your stomach. You run to the kitchen and scan the contents of the pantry and fridge. Your options are scarce, but you are hopeful. You frantically search high and low, pushing aside out-of-date tin cans and condiments. You fail to find anything delicious. You drop your shoulders in anguish and walk back to the couch, hungry and hurt.

I've got you.

This chapter is all about tasty snacks that you can make with staple and overlooked ingredients. Recipes such as Puff Pastry Pizzas, Sweet and Spicy Anything Mix and Tony Pepperoni Chips. You will be surprised by what you can whip up on a whim!

PUFF PASTRY PIZZAS

A great recipe for kids who want a quick snack.

Makes 4
1 sheet puff pastry, thawed
4 tablespoons pizza sauce
4 slices deli ham
⅓ cup diced pineapple
½ cup bocconcini

- On a dry surface, cut the puff pastry sheet into four equal pieces. *(You can make four small pizzas like this or you can make one big pizza buy cutting the pastry into a circle the same diameter as your air fryer.)*
- Preheat air fryer to 180°C.
- On each piece, spoon a tablespoon of pizza sauce and spread evenly over the pastry. Tear the ham slices in half and place two halves on each piece of pastry. Evenly distribute the pineapple pieces over the pizzas. Tear the bocconcini in halves and evenly distribute them over the pizzas.
- Line the preheated air fryer basket with baking paper then place two of the pizzas into the air fryer. Cook at 180°C for 7–10 minutes, until cheese is melted and pastry is golden and cooked through. Repeat with the remaining two pizzas.

BACON-WRAPPED ONION RINGS

Sometimes I wish I was wrapped in bacon.

Makes 8
1 large onion
8 rashers streaky bacon

- On a cutting board, cut off the top and bottom of the onion and then peel it. Slice the onion into 1 cm thick round slices. *(Don't cry, it's only an onion.)* Push the centres out of the slices, keeping the large outside rings. You will need eight large rings. *(There will be some leftover onion. If you don't want to throw it out, you can store it in the fridge for another time.)*
- Take a rasher of bacon and carefully wrap it around and around an onion ring. This can be slightly tricky with regular bacon, so make sure you have streaky bacon. Once the onion is fully wrapped in bacon, secure it with a toothpick. Repeat with the remaining bacon and onion rings.
- Preheat air fryer to 200°C.
- Place the bacon-wrapped onion rings into the air fryer in a single layer *(you may have to cook them in batches, depending on the size of your air fryer)* and cook at 200°C for 10–12 minutes or until the bacon has reached your desired crispiness. *(I like my bacon half crispy, half chewy.)*
- Enjoy with dipping sauce of your choice.

SWEET AND SPICY ANYTHING MIX

A great way to turn regular old pantry items into an exciting snack.

Serves 3–4

2 cups dried small pasta (farfalle/bowties are ideal; anything long like
   spaghetti won't work)
2 tablespoons brown sugar
2 teaspoons smoked paprika
1 teaspoon onion powder
1 teaspoon garlic powder
½ teaspoon chilli powder
¼ cup olive oil
½ cup cashews
½ cup almonds
1 cup pretzels
1 cup Kellogg's Nutri-Grain
1 teaspoon salt

- Cook pasta as per packet instructions. *(I'll give you a hint: you have to cook it in boiling water.)* Once cooked, drain well, then pat dry with paper towel. Pour into a large bowl.
- In a small bowl, add sugar, paprika, onion powder, garlic powder, chilli powder and oil. Stir to combine. Spoon half the mixture over the pasta and toss to coat.
- Preheat air fryer to 200°C.
- Place the seasoned pasta into the air fryer and cook at 200°C for 10 minutes, stirring halfway, until golden and crispy. Remove pasta from air fryer and transfer to a large bowl. Reduce air fryer temperature to 180°C.

- Add nuts and pretzels to another bowl. Coat and toss with remaining seasoning mixture.
- Place nuts and pretzels into air fryer basket and cook at 180°C for 6 minutes, stirring halfway.
- Add cooked nuts and pretzels, Nutri-Grain and salt to pasta, then toss to combine.
- Let the mix cool completely before serving.

♫ *You get your leftovers out of the fridge doodloodoo* ♪

TONY PEPPERONI CHIPS

Crispy little pepperonis that even the keto fans will enjoy.

Makes as many as you like
cooking oil spray
pepperoni slices (as many as you desire)

- Preheat air fryer to 200°C.
- Spray the base of the basket of the air fryer with cooking oil spray.
- Add the pepperoni to the air fryer. They don't need to be in a single layer, just throw them in.
- Cook at 200°C for 10 minutes or until they become golden. They won't be crispy until they cool down so don't worry if they are still floppy.
- Place on a paper towel-lined tray and let cool completely before serving.

RAVIOLI CHIPS

Rodney reluctantly ravaged the remaining ravioli. Rude, Rodney, really rude!

Serves 2
200 g beef ravioli
3 tablespoons olive oil
1 teaspoon dried Italian seasoning
1 teaspoon garlic powder
1 teaspoon onion powder
¼ teaspoon chilli flakes
20 g parmesan cheese, grated

- In a large pot, cook the ravioli as per packet instructions. Be careful not to overcook; you want the ravioli to remain slightly firm. Drain well and pat down with paper towel. Transfer to a large bowl.
- Add olive oil, Italian seasoning *(or any seasoning you prefer)*, garlic powder, onion powder, chilli flakes and parmesan cheese. Toss well to combine.
- Preheat air fryer to 200°C.
- Add seasoned ravioli to the air fryer and cook at 200°C for 10 minutes, tossing halfway, until golden and crispy.
- Serve warm and try dipping the ravioli chips into some Napoletana sauce.

CHEESY BOLOGNAISE PASTIES

These are ideal if you have leftover bolognaise. In case you don't, this recipe has got you covered.

Makes 6
1 tablespoon olive oil
1 large onion, diced
4 cloves garlic, diced
500 g beef mince
1 tablespoon tomato paste
1 tablespoon Italian seasoning
400 g can diced tomatoes
3 sheets puff pastry, thawed
1 cup grated cheese
2 eggs, beaten
1 tablespoon sesame seeds

- Heat olive oil in medium-sized saucepan over medium-high heat. Add diced onion and sauté for 5 minutes or until softened. Add diced garlic and cook for 1 minute or until fragrant. Add beef mince and cook until browned. Add tomato paste and Italian seasoning and stir well to combine, then add diced tomatoes. Bring to a boil then reduce heat to low and simmer, covered, for 10–15 minutes, stirring occasionally.
- Once cooked, transfer bolognaise to a bowl and put it in the freezer for 20–30 minutes. *(If you are using leftover bolognaise, you can skip this step because your sauce will already be cool. The bolognaise needs to be completely cooled before adding to the pastry.)*

- Meanwhile, lay your pastry sheets out onto a dry surface. Cut pastry into 15 cm rounds. *(I like to place a small bowl upside down onto the pastry then cut around it with a sharp knife.)* Remove any excess pastry and transfer the rounds onto a piece of baking paper.
- Remove the bowl of bolognaise from the freezer. Add cheese and stir to combine.
- Scoop some of the bolognaise mixture into the centre of a pastry round and brush the edges with a little bit of beaten egg. Lift the two halves of the circle together and pinch to make a pasty. Brush the top of the pasty with egg and sprinkle with a pinch of sesame seeds. Repeat with the remaining ingredients.
- Preheat air fryer to 200°C.
- Line the preheated air fryer basket with baking paper. Place pasties into the air fryer in a single layer, cooking in batches at 200°C for 13–15 minutes, until the pastry is golden and flaky, the filling is heated, and the cheese is oozing.

CHEESY VEGEMITE ROLL UPS

I love these little suckers!

Makes 12
2 sheets puff pastry
2 tablespoons Vegemite
1 cup grated cheese
1 egg, beaten

- Lay out the frozen puff pastry sheets onto a flat surface lined with baking paper. Evenly spread 1 tablespoon of Vegemite over each piece of pastry then let it thaw to room temperature.
- Sprinkle grated cheese evenly over both sheets of pastry. Cut each sheet into thirds lengthwise, then roll up each third, until you have six long pastry roll ups. Cut the roll ups in half so you have twelve pieces, then use a sharp knife to gently score the roll ups *(just make a two or three incisions into the top of the roll ups, making sure not to cut all the way through)*. Brush the roll ups with beaten egg.
- Preheat air fryer to 200°C.
- Line the air fryer with baking paper, then place half the roll ups into the air fryer. Cook at 200°C for 10 minutes or until the pastry is golden and flaky and the cheese oozing. Repeat with remaining rollups.
- Serve warm or at room temperature.

MUM'S CHEESE AND BACON QUICHE PUFFS

My mum makes these all the time for us. This is her secret recipe (sorry, Mum).

Makes 24
3 sheets puff pastry, thawed
1 tablespoon butter, melted
24 patty pans
8 rashers bacon
1 onion, finely chopped
1 cup grated cheese
2 eggs
1 cup milk
1 tablespoon chopped fresh parsley
pinch salt and pepper

- Place the thawed pastry onto a dry surface. Cut into 8 cm rounds. Brush melted butter inside patty pans then press pastry rounds inside.
- Remove rind from bacon and chop into small pieces.
- In a frying pan over medium–high heat, add bacon and chopped onion. Fry until bacon is crisp and onion is tender. Remove from heat and let cool.
- Spoon a small amount of bacon mixture into each of the pastry cases. Top with a sprinkle of grated cheese.
- Preheat air fryer to 200°C.
- Whisk eggs and milk in a bowl until combined. Add parsley and salt and pepper then mix to combine. Spoon enough egg mixture over each pastry to cover the bacon filling.
- In batches, place the quiches into the air fryer. Cook at 200°C for 5 minutes then reduce heat to 160°C and cook for a further 5–7 minutes or until quiches are golden brown.

SIZZLER COPYCAT TOAST

I used to love going to Sizzler as a kid for two reasons. One, I have always had a huge appetite and loved the all-you-can-eat buffet and two, I loved that free piece of cheese toast you received when you ordered the salad bar.

Makes 4
½ loaf unsliced white bread
⅓ cup unsalted butter, softened
½ cup grated parmesan cheese

- Use a bread knife to cut the loaf into four even thick slices. Discard the end piece *(or as I like to call it, the butt)*.
- In a small bowl, add butter and parmesan cheese. Mix thoroughly to combine.
- Spread the butter mix evenly over each of the four pieces of bread, top and bottom.
- Preheat air fryer to 200°C.
- Place buttered bread into the air fryer, two pieces at a time. Cook at 200°C for 4–5 minutes, then flip and cook for a further 2–3 minutes, until both sides are golden and crispy.

CHICKEN SALT TORTILLA CHIPS

Australians love chicken salt, but we usually have it on hot chips. You have to try these chicken salt tortilla chips.

Serves 2
8 soft corn tortillas
cooking oil spray
1 tablespoon chicken salt

- Preheat air fryer to 190°C.
- Spray both sides of the tortillas with a generous amount of cooking oil spray. Cut each tortilla into six triangles. *(This recipe works better if the tortillas are dry and a bit stale, so no need to throw out those old tortillas any more.)*
- Spray the base of the air fryer basket with cooking oil spray then arrange the triangles in a single layer in the air fryer. *(You will have to cook the chips in batches.)*
- Cook at 190°C for 10 minutes or until the chips are crisp and golden brown. Remove from air fryer and transfer to a large bowl. Repeat with remaining tortilla triangles.
- Once all the chips are cooked, add chicken salt and toss to combine.
- Enjoy!

CHEESE AND ONION RINGS

These guys are slightly tricky to put together, but they are well worth the effort.

Makes 6
2 large white onions
3 slices cheese (I like to use Swiss or mozzarella, but any cheese
   will do)
1 cup plain flour
3 eggs, beaten
1 cup panko breadcrumbs
½ teaspoon salt
½ teaspoon pepper
cooking oil spray

- Peel and cut onions into 1 cm thick rings.
- Cut each slice of cheese into four even strips.
- Place a smaller onion ring into the centre of a larger onion ring, so there is a small gap between them.
- Fill the gap between the onion rings with cheese strips. *(You should be able to fit two strips inside the onion ring.)*
- Place flour, beaten eggs and breadcrumbs into three separate bowls. Add salt and pepper to the flour and mix to combine. Dip a cheese-filled onion ring into the flour. Shake off any excess then dip into the egg. Finally, dip the ring into the breadcrumbs and coat completely. Set aside and repeat with the remaining rings.
- Preheat air fryer to 180°C.
- Spray the preheated air fryer basket with cooking oil spray. Place some of the onion rings into the air fryer in a single layer. Spray generously with cooking oil spray and cook at 180°C for 7–10 minutes, flipping halfway, until golden brown and the cheese is oozing. Repeat with remaining onion rings.
- Serve with marinara dipping sauce.

LEXI'S CRISPY CHEESE BITES

Every time I make these, one of my doggos, Lexi, comes running into the kitchen and waits patiently for her share. They are great for humans, too.

Serves 2–4

1 cup grated cheese
2 tablespoons butter, cold
¼ teaspoon salt
⅛ teaspoon onion powder
⅛ teaspoon garlic powder
½ cup plain flour
2–3 tablespoons water

- Add grated cheese, butter, salt, onion powder and garlic powder to a food processor and combine. (*If you don't have a food processor you can use a handheld mixer or combine by hand, but I don't recommend doing it by hand.*)
- Once combined, gradually mix in the flour until the mixture turns into breadcrumbs.
- Add 2 tablespoons water and mix further until the mixture turns into dough. This process should take a few minutes. Add another tablespoon of water if the dough feels too dry.
- Divide the dough into three pieces, then roll each piece into the shape of a log. Cover with cling wrap and refrigerate for 2 hours.
- Preheat air fryer to 180°C.
- Remove dough from fridge and cut the logs into 0.5 cm slices. Place the slices onto a piece of baking paper.
- Line the air fryer basket with baking paper and add a single layer of cheese bites. In batches, cook at 180°C for 10–12 minutes or until they are medium golden brown. Repeat with remaining cheese bites and serve.

TONY K'S CRUSTY PICKLES

Tony K's crusty pickles are mouth-watering :)

Serves 4–6
1 small jar sliced dill pickles
1 cup plain flour
1 teaspoon fajita seasoning
2 eggs, beaten
1 cup panko breadcrumbs
cooking oil spray

- Drain pickles well and place onto a paper towel-lined plate. Pat dry completely with paper towel. (*You don't have to use the whole jar of pickles, just use as many as you feel like.*)
- Set out three bowls. In the first add flour and fajita seasoning, then mix to combine. Add beaten egg to the second bowl and breadcrumbs to the third.
- Dip the pickles into the flour, a few at a time. Then dip into the egg and finally into the breadcrumbs. Dip the crumbed pickles back into the egg and then again into the breadcrumbs. Set aside and repeat with remaining pickles.
- Preheat air fryer to 200°C.
- Spray air fryer basket with cooking oil spray and place the pickles into the air fryer in a single layer. Cook in batches at 200°C for 8 minutes, turning halfway, until golden.
- Enjoy!

BERRY NICE PIES

One of my favourite desserts. The glaze tastes just like Krispy Kreme.

Makes 12
4 sheets shortcrust pastry, thawed
415 g can black cherries in syrup
2 cups icing sugar
¼ cup milk

- On a dry surface, cut 10 cm circles out of the shortcrust pastry. You should get three circles per sheet. *(If you don't have a cookie cutter that size, use a small bowl and cut around the edge to make a circle.)*
- Add a heaped tablespoon of cherries to the centre of each circle.
- Moisten the edges of the circle with a little bit of water, then fold over one side, making a semicircle. Press down on the edges to seal in the cherries. *(Don't worry if some of the cherry filling comes out.)* Crimp the outside edges using the end of a fork and poke a couple of holes into the top of the pie with a toothpick.
- Preheat air fryer to 190°C.
- Line the air fryer basket with baking paper and place four pies into the air fryer. Cook at 190°C for 7–9 minutes or until pies are golden brown. Repeat with remaining pies.
- Meanwhile, whisk the icing sugar and milk in a large bowl until it becomes a smooth glaze.
- One at a time, dip each pie into the glaze, making sure to completely cover it, and set aside on a sheet of baking paper. Let the pies cool and set for at least 15 minutes before serving.

BAKED BEAN TOAST PARCELS

Baked beans make you f ... f ... feel really good.

Makes 2

4 slices bread

220 g can baked beans (I like the ones in ham sauce)

½ cup grated cheese

2 tablespoons butter, melted

- Cut the crusts off the bread. Use your fingers to gently press down the centre of two of the slices, forming a little indent.
- Spoon baked beans into the indents and top with grated cheese, making sure the cheese and beans aren't touching the edges of the bread. Place the other slices of bread on top and firmly press around the edges to seal.
- Brush both bread parcels, top and bottom, with butter.
- Preheat air fryer to 180°C.
- Air fry the parcels at 180°C for 5–7 minutes or until golden.

DAD'S LITTLE BOYS IN BACON

My dad has been hounding me to make this recipe for a while.
Nice one, Dad.

Makes 12
6 rashers streaky bacon
12 cocktail frankfurts
¼ cup mayonnaise
1 tablespoon sriracha

- Preheat air fryer to 180°C.
- Cut bacon rashers in half.
- Wrap each frankfurt with half a rasher of bacon and secure it with a toothpick.
- Place the bacon-wrapped frankfurts into the air fryer in a single layer and cook at 180°C for 7–10 minutes or until the bacon reaches your desired crispiness. Repeat with remaining frankfurts.
- Meanwhile, add mayonnaise and sriracha to a small bowl and stir to combine.
- Serve frankfurts with spicy mayo dipping sauce.

ROYAL PASTRY BOMBS

Chocolate, jam, marshmallow and biscuit pastries that are so delicious you'll have to hide them from your family.

Makes 8
4 sheets puff pastry, thawed
8 Arnott's Royals biscuits
2 tablespoon unsalted butter, melted
1 tablespoon icing sugar

- Cut out 8–10 cm circles from the puff pastry. *(You can use the base of a bowl or the outside of a cup as a guide.)* You will need a total of sixteen circles.
- Place a Royal into the centre of eight of the circles.
- Wet your finger with some water and moisten the outside edges of the pastry circles. Place the remaining pastry circles on top of the Royals and apply pressure to the edges to seal. Use a fork to crimp the edges, further sealing them. Poke a few holes in the top of the pastries with a toothpick.
- Preheat air fryer to 190°C.
- Brush melted butter over the pastries.
- Line the air fryer basket with baking paper and place two or three pastries inside. Cook at 190°C for 7–10 minutes or until golden and flaky. Repeat with remaining pastries.
- Dust pastries with icing sugar before serving.

CHILLI LIME CRISPY CHICKPEAS

Easy and healthy with a nice little kick.

Serves 2–3
400 g can chickpeas
cooking oil spray
½ teaspoon chilli powder
½ teaspoon cumin
½ teaspoon salt
½ teaspoon garlic powder
zest of 1 lime

- Preheat air fryer to 200°C.
- Drain chickpeas then place in the air fryer and cook at 200°C for 5 minutes. Open air fryer and spray with cooking oil. Give the basket a shake and cook for a further 5 minutes, shake basket again, then another 5 minutes.
- Meanwhile, in a small bowl, add chilli powder, cumin, salt, garlic powder and lime zest and stir to combine. *(Feel free to use any spice combination, like BBQ or even cinnamon sugar.)* Sprinkle half the spice mixture onto the chickpeas and cook for a further 2 minutes.
- Place chickpeas in a bowl and sprinkle with the remaining spice mixture. Stir to combine and serve.

BACON JALAPEÑO POPPERS

I firmly believe that everything is better when you add bacon.

Makes 12
6 fresh jalapeños
150 g block cream cheese
½ teaspoon garlic powder
1 spring onion, finely chopped
⅓ cup grated cheese
12 rashers streaky bacon

- Cut each jalapeño in half lengthwise. Remove stems and scrape out seeds. *(Be careful not to touch your eyes after handling jalapeños.)*
- In a small bowl, add cream cheese *(make sure it's block cream cheese; the spreadable kind isn't ideal)*, garlic powder, spring onion and grated cheese. Mix together to combine then stuff the cheese mixture into the jalapeño halves.
- Wrap the stuffed jalapeños with bacon, making sure to completely cover the cheese. Secure with toothpicks.
- Preheat air fryer to 200°C.
- Place half the jalapeños into the air fryer and cook at 200°C for 15 minutes or until the bacon is cooked to your liking and the cheese is oozing. Remove from air fryer and repeat with the remaining jalapeños.

AVOCADO FRIES

On average, I eat an avocado a day. This recipe is a different way to eat an avocado.

Serves 3–4
2–3 avocados
1 cup panko breadcrumbs
½ cup grated parmesan cheese
½ teaspoon pepper
2 eggs, beaten
cooking oil spray
pinch salt

- Peel avocados and remove seeds. *(The easiest way to peel an avocado is to cut it in half, then cut a small section off the top and bottom of the avocado. The skin will peel off easily.)* Cut each avocado half into about four slices lengthwise.
- Set out two medium-sized bowls. In the first bowl, add breadcrumbs, parmesan cheese and pepper then mix to combine. Add beaten egg to the second bowl.
- Dip the avocado slices into the egg, then into the crumb mixture and coat completely.
- Preheat air fryer to 180°C.
- Spray the preheated air fryer basket with cooking oil spray and place avocado slices into the air fryer in a single layer, making sure they aren't touching each other. Cook in batches at 180°C for 6 minutes, turning halfway, until golden brown.

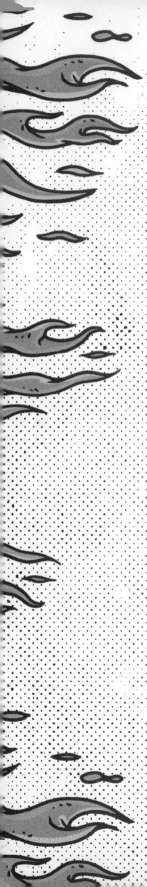

DON'T TRY THIS AT HOME!

If you are feeling a bit experimental and want to try something that is a bit left of field, this chapter is for you. I've tried making some weird creations in the air fryer; some of them work and some of them don't. That's what I love about cooking. So get out of your comfort zone and try my Panko-Crumbed Potato Salad Sandwich, or the weird and wonderful Mango Fries. You just might be inspired to create something different.

DEN'S FORBIDDEN FRUIT

This is how you turn a regular old apple into a more than a regular old apple.

Makes 4
2 apples (Pink Lady are my favourite)
1 tablespoon melted butter
¼ teaspoon cinnamon
3 tablespoons brown sugar
pinch salt
2 tablespoons rolled oats

- Cut apples in half through the stem.
- Use a spoon or small knife to scoop out the core, seeds and some of the apple flesh. *(Keep the flesh separate from the core and seeds.)* Make sure you make a cavity big enough to hold the sugar filling.
- Dice the scooped-out flesh into small pieces. You should have just under a cup of diced apple. *(If you need more, just scoop some more out from the apples.)*
- In a medium-sized bowl, combine melted butter, cinnamon, brown sugar and salt. Then stir in chopped apple and oats.
- Lightly pack a quarter of the filling into each apple half.
- Pour ½ cup water into the air fryer *(this will keep the apple really moist and texturally delicious)*. Place apple halves into the air fryer, filling side up. Make sure they don't wobble too much. *(If you feel like they might tip over, take them out of the air fryer and firmly press them onto a flat surface to flatten the bottom slightly.)*
- Cook at 180°C for 12–15 minutes or until the filling is golden brown and the apple is cooked through.
- Serve hot with a dollop of vanilla ice cream.

PANKO-CRUMBED POTATO SALAD SANDWICH

Why is there always leftover potato salad in the fridge after a party? This recipe was inspired by a video I saw of a Korean street food chef making crumbed potato salad croquettes. When I first made it, I only had a little bit of potato salad so I turned it into a sandwich to keep those pesky tummy grumbles away.

Makes 1

2 slices white bread
½ cup potato salad
1 slice tasty cheese
½ cup plain flour
1 egg, beaten
½ cup panko breadcrumbs

- Place bread onto a flat surface. Scoop potato salad onto one slice and spread evenly. Place a slice of cheese on top of the other slice. *(You can stop there if you want a nice regular sandwich without any risks. But if you want to pimp your sandwich, keep reading.)*
- Add flour to one medium-sized bowl, beaten egg to another and breadcrumbs to a third.
- Dip sandwich into the flour until covered *(make sure you cover the outside edges to seal in the filling)*. Shake off excess flour then dip into egg, then into breadcrumbs. *(The sandwich should be completely sealed, so you shouldn't be able to see any filling. The idea is to keep the cheese inside so it doesn't ooze out while cooking.)*
- Preheat air fryer to 180°C.
- Spay the base of the air fryer basket with cooking spray and place sandwich inside.
- Cook at 180°C for 10–12 minutes, flipping halfway, until golden brown. *(If a little bit of cheese is oozing out then it's a good sign its ready.)*

MANGO FRIES

Yes, you read correctly. It's just as weird as you can imagine, but oddly delicious.

Serves 1–2
1 (almost ripe) mango
¼ cup plain flour
½ teaspoon chilli powder
pinch salt
cooking oil spray

- Peel mango with a potato peeler. Using a sharp knife, cut the mango on both sides of the seed. Discard seed. Place mango halves face down onto a chopping board and slice into 1.5 cm thick slices.
- In a medium-sized bowl, add flour, chilli powder (*if you don't like spice you can use paprika*) and salt.
- Lightly coat each slice of mango with the flour mixture and shake of any excess.
- Preheat air fryer to 200°C.
- Spray the air fryer basket with the cooking oil spray and place the mango slices inside making sure they are not touching. (*You may have to cook in batches, depending on the size of your air fryer.*)
- Cook at 200°C for 10 minutes, turning halfway, until mango fries are crispy.

REDHOT HALLOUMI STICKS

I love halloumi! These little beauties are a great. Spicy and cheesy!

Serves 1–2
180 g halloumi
1 egg
⅓ cup Frank's RedHot Sauce
1 cup plain flour
1 cup panko breadcrumbs
cooking oil spray

- On a chopping board, slice halloumi into 1 cm thick slices. (*You can cut them into any size or shape you like. You could even leave it whole if you are a risk-taker.*)
- In a medium-sized bowl, add egg and hot sauce and whisk to combine.
- Add flour to another bowl and breadcrumbs to a third.
- One by one, dip the halloumi slices into the flour and shake off any excess. Then coat in the egg mixture before covering in breadcrumbs.
- Preheat air fryer to 200°C.
- Spray the base of the air fryer basket with cooking oil spray.
- Place the crumbed halloumi into the air fryer, making sure to leave a 1 cm gap between each piece.
- Cook at 200°C for 7–10 minutes, turning halfway, until golden brown and crisp.
- Serve with bacon and eggs or sautéed mushrooms, spinach and toast. Or all of the above.

RAMEN PANCAKE

I'm a sucker for ramen. I could eat it every day. There are so many ways to make it that it's impossible to get bored of. You just have to use your imagination.

Makes 1
1 packet of your favourite ramen
1 egg, beaten

- Boil 500 ml of water in a medium-sized saucepan.
- Add ramen and soup powder to the boiling water and cook for 4 minutes (*or follow the instructions on the back of the packet*).
- Once noodles are cooked, drain well and add to the beaten egg. Mix until combined.
- Preheat air fryer to 180°C.
- Cut out a piece of baking paper just smaller than the circumference of your air fryer basket and place it inside. Pour the ramen and egg mixture onto the paper, making sure it doesn't spill over the edges.
- Cook at 180°C for 5–7 minutes, turning halfway, until golden and crunchy.

CHICKEN-TWISTIES CHICKEN

You can tell a lot about a person by their choice of Twisties flavour. Cheese Twisties people love the classics, while Chicken Twisties people are risk-takers. Which one are you? Cheese or chicken? I'm a Chicken Twistie guy. If you are undecided, this recipe might help.

Makes 2

1 chicken breast
1 small bag (90 g) chicken-flavoured Twisties
½ cup plain flour
1 egg, beaten
cooking oil spray

- Using a sharp knife, cut the chicken breast in half by slicing parallel with the bench, so that you end up with two thinner pieces. Set aside.
- Empty the Twisties into a ziplock bag, remove excess air and seal. Use a rolling pin to crush the Twisties into small crumbs and add them to a small bowl.
- Add flour to another small bowl and beaten egg to a third.
- Dip the chicken into the flour, covering all sides and shaking off any excess. Then dip into the egg mixture, before covering with Twisties crumbs. Press the chicken firmly into the Twisties to help the crumbs stick to the chicken.
- Preheat air fryer to 200°C.
- Spray the base of the air fryer basket with cooking oil spray, then lay the crumbed chicken inside before spraying the chicken with a little more cooking oil spray.
- Cook chicken at 200°C for 8 minutes, turning halfway, until golden and crunchy. Make sure the chicken is fully cooked before serving.

SURPRISE PIE

When it comes to air frying, puff pastry is one of the most versatile ingredients. You can basically wrap anything in a bit of pastry and it tastes good.

Makes 1

1 Kinder Surprise egg
2 tablespoons Nutella
2 marshmallows
1 sheet puff pastry, thawed
1 tablespoon unsalted butter, melted

- Unwrap Kinder Surprise egg and gently squeeze the egg so that it separates cleanly into two halves. Discard toy. (*Do not eat the toy, LOL!*)
- Spoon 1 tablespoon Nutella into each egg half. Then firmly push a marshmallow into each half. Dip your finger into some warm water and run your finger around the edge of each egg. Reconnect the egg together by softly pressing both halves back together.
- Preheat air fryer to 180°C.
- Place the pastry onto a dry surface. Find a small heat-proof bowl or silicone pie tin approximately 10 cm in diameter and place upside down onto the pastry. Use a sharp knife to cut around the bowl. Repeat to make two pastry circles.
- Grease the inside and top edges of the bowl with melted butter. Place a pastry circle inside the bowl, pushing it into the bowl shape, and place the Nutella-filled egg inside.

- Dip your finger into some water and run it around the outside edge of the remaining piece of pastry. Place this pastry, wet side down, on top of the egg. Secure the pieces of pastry together by pressing firmly around the edges. Brush the top with remaining butter.
- Place the pie into the air fryer and cook at 180°C for 10 minutes or until the pastry is golden and flaky.
- Remove the pie from the air fryer and let it cool in the dish for 5 minutes.
- Gently remove the pie from the dish and serve with vanilla ice cream.

♫ *Kinder Surprise will open your eyes. when it's filled with Nutella and fun!* ♫

SNICKERS WONTONS

What's in your wonton?

Makes 8
2 (50 g) Snickers bars
8 wonton wrappers
cooking oil spray

- Place Snickers bars onto a chopping board and cut into quarters as evenly as possible. Once cut, firmly press down on each piece to slightly flatten.
- Fill a small bowl with some lukewarm water.
- Place a wonton wrapper onto a dry surface. Place a piece of Snickers into the centre of the wrapper. Dip your finger into the water and gently run it around the outside edges of the wrapper. Fold the wrapper over to make a triangle and gently press the edges together to seal. Repeat with the remaining wrappers and Snickers.
- Preheat air fryer to 180°C.
- Spray the base of the air fryer basket with cooking oil spray. Place the wontons into the air fryer in a single layer, cooking in batches if they do not all fit. Spray wontons with more cooking oil spray.
- Cook at 180°C for 7–10 minutes or until crispy and golden.
- Rest for a few minutes before serving with a scoop of your favourite ice cream.

♫ *You put the snickers on the pastry* ♪
HELL YEAH ♫

SALAMI STACKS

Stacks of cheese and salami.

Serves 3–4

200 g Swiss cheese slices
100 g mild Hungarian salami
1 cup plain flour
2 eggs, beaten
1 cup panko breadcrumbs
cooking oil spray

- Place cheese slices onto a chopping board. Use a sharp knife to cut the slices into quarters. *(Now it's time to make the stacks.)*
- First, place a slice of salami onto a flat surface. Then top with a piece of cheese. Then layer with salami, then cheese, then salami again. Secure with a toothpick. Repeat these steps with the remaining salami and cheese. *(Each stack should have three pieces of salami and two pieces of cheese.)*
- Preheat air fryer to 180°C.
- Set out three small bowls. Add flour to the first bowl, beaten eggs to the second and breadcrumbs to the third.
- Dip the salami stacks, one by one, into the flour. Shake off any excess then dip into the egg. Finally, drop the stacks into the breadcrumbs and cover completely.
- Spray the base of the air fryer basket with cooking oil spray and place the stacks into the air fryer in a single layer. *(You may have to cook them in two batches.)* Spray the stacks with a little bit more cooking oil spray and cook at 180°C for 5–7 minutes, or until golden and cheese is oozing.
- Serve as an appetiser or afternoon snack.

CRUMBED EGGPLANT PIZZA

Is there a better alternative to pizza? Probably not. But these eggplant pizzas are just as good and feel guilt-free.

Serves 2–4

1 eggplant
1 cup panko breadcrumbs
½ cup parmesan cheese, grated
1 teaspoon garlic powder
2 teaspoons Italian seasoning
¼ teaspoon salt
¼ teaspoon pepper
¼ cup parsley, finely chopped
½ cup plain flour
2 eggs, beaten
cooking oil spray
½ cup pizza sauce
200 g pepperoni slices
200 g bocconcini cheese

- Cut eggplant into 1 cm thick rounds. (*If you have extra time and want creamier tasting eggplant, you can salt it before cooking. Sprinkle salt over the cut sides of the eggplant and rest for 30 minutes, then rinse and pat dry.*)
- In a small bowl, combine breadcrumbs, parmesan cheese, garlic powder, Italian seasoning, salt, pepper and parsley. Add flour to another bowl and beaten eggs to a third.

- One by one, dip eggplant rounds into the flour and shake off excess. Then dip into the egg. *(Make sure to coat both sides so there are no dry areas.)* Then press the eggplant into the breadcrumb mixture, coating both sides and edges. Set aside and repeat with the remaining rounds.
- Preheat air fryer to 180°C.
- Spray cooking oil on both sides of the eggplant rounds and onto the base of the air fryer basket. Cook in batches at 180°C for 5 minutes, then flip and cook for a further 5 minutes, until golden. Remove eggplant rounds from air fryer and set on a baking sheet or plate.
- Once all rounds are cooked, increase air fryer temperature to 200°C.
- Spread pizza sauce over each eggplant round. Top with pepperoni. Break bocconcini into smaller pieces and place on top of the eggplant pizzas. *(You can add any pizza topping you like.)*
- Transfer pizzas back into air fryer and cook at 200°C for a further 3 minutes or until cheese has melted, then serve hot.

PEANUT BUTTER JALAPEÑO POPPERS

It sounds weird but tastes less weird.

Makes 6
6 fresh jalapeño peppers
6 tablespoons smooth peanut butter
1 cup plain flour
1 egg, beaten
1 cup panko breadcrumbs
cooking oil spray

- Use a sharp knife to cut the peppers in half lengthwise. Scrape out any seeds with a teaspoon.
- Using a butter knife, fill each half with peanut butter. *(You might need more peanut butter if you have large jalapeños.)* Reconnect the jalapeño halves back together, securing with a toothpick.
- Preheat air fryer to 180°C.
- Set out three small bowls. Add flour to the first bowl, beaten egg to the second and breadcrumbs to the third.
- One by one, dip the peanut butter-filled peppers into the flour. Shake off any excess then dip into the egg. Finally, drop the peppers into the breadcrumbs and cover completely.
- Spray the base of the air fryer basket with cooking oil spray and place the jalapeño poppers into the air fryer in a single layer.
- Spray with a little bit more cooking oil spray and cook at 180°C for 7–10 minutes, or until golden and crispy.

PEAR IN THE HOLE

Sweet and dangerous.

Makes 4
3 tablespoons butter, melted
3 tablespoons brown sugar
½ teaspoon ground cinnamon
¼ teaspoon ground nutmeg
2 pears

- In a small bowl, combine melted butter, sugar, cinnamon and nutmeg.
- Preheat air fryer to 160°C.
- Cut pears in half and remove core with a teaspoon. *(You can also peel the pears if you like, but I prefer to keep the skin on because it creates a different texture.)* Place the pear halves into the butter spice mixture and cover completely. Keep the remaining butter spice mixture for a later step.
- Place some baking paper into the base of the air fryer basket.
- Place the pears onto the baking paper, flat side down, and cook at 160°C for 10 minutes. Flip the pears and drizzle with the remaining butter spice mixture and cook for 2–4 more minutes, until they start to caramelise.
- Serve warm with ice cream.

HASH BROWN PARMI

Parmi or parma? How about potatarmi?

Makes 1
2 medium brushed potatoes
¼ cup passata
½ tablespoon Italian herbs
cooking oil spray
salt and pepper to taste
2 slices ham
2 slices swiss cheese

- Peel and wash the potatoes. Lay a clean tea towel onto a flat surface and grate the potatoes, using the large holes of a cheese grater, directly onto the towel. Tightly wrap the tea towel around the potatoes and squeeze the moisture out. Work in batches to make it less of a physical challenge. *(Potatoes can sometimes stain tea towels so don't use one of your fancy ones.)*
- Preheat air fryer to 200°C.
- In a small bowl, combine passata and herbs. *(You could use pre-made pasta sauce instead.)*
- Place a piece of baking paper into the air fryer basket and spray with a generous amount of cooking oil spray. Put the drained grated potato onto the greased paper and flatten it down with your hand to 1 cm thick. Sprinkle some salt and pepper over the hash brown then spray it with more cooking oil spray.
- Cook at 200°C for 5–7 minutes or until the top of the hash brown is golden brown. Use a large spatula to flip the hash brown over.
- Spoon the passata sauce over the hash brown and spread evenly. Top with ham and cheese.
- Cook at 200°C for another 2–3 minutes or until the cheese is melted.
- Serve for breakfast or dinner!

LEFTOVER CURRY SPRING ROLLS

I make these for dinner the night after having Indian food. They are a great way to stretch out those leftovers.

Makes 6

6 spring roll wrappers, thawed
1 cup leftover curry and rice
cooking oil spray

- Remove last night's curry and rice from the fridge and stir to combine. It's good to have about half rice, half curry, but any combination will do.
- On a dry surface, place a spring roll wrapper *(smooth side down)* in a diamond position. Place a heaped dessertspoon of curry filling on the bottom corner of the wrapper. Roll the wrapper up halfway, fold sides in, then finish rolling. Dip your finger into some water and lightly moisten the last flap of the wrapper then lightly press along the seal until it sticks. Repeat with the remaining wrappers.
- Preheat air fryer to 190°C.
- Spray spring rolls with a generous amount of cooking oil spray.
- Place spring rolls into the air fryer and cook at 190°C for 7–10 minutes or until the pastry is golden and crunchy.

CHIP OFF THE OLD BLOCK

If you aren't scared of calories, this one's for you.

Serves 4

2 sheets puff pastry, thawed
1 block (180 g) chocolate (I like to use a block of Cadbury Top Deck
    but you can use any block you like)
2 tablespoons butter, melted
1 teaspoon icing sugar (optional)

- Place thawed pastry onto a dry surface.
- Remove chocolate from wrapper *(very important, LOL)* and place the whole block of chocolate into the centre of one of the pastry sheets. Then place the other pastry sheet on top. Run your finger around the edges to secure the pastry sheets together.
- Cut away excess pastry, leaving approximately 1 cm of pastry around the chocolate. Use a fork to press down around the edges of the pastry to secure further. Poke a few holes into the top of the pastry with a toothpick.
- Preheat air fryer to 180°C.
- Brush the chocolate pastry with melted butter.
- Place a sheet of baking paper into the base of the air fryer basket then place the pastry inside.
- Cook at 180°C for 8–10 minutes or until pastry is golden and chocolate is melted in the centre.
- Let pastry cool slightly before dusting with icing sugar, then slice and serve.

PIMPED LEFTOVER LASAGNE

Leftover lasagne like you have never seen before.

Serves 2

2 pieces leftover lasagne, cold (roughly the size of a slice of cheese)
4 slices cheese
½ cup plain flour
2 eggs, beaten
1 cup panko breadcrumbs
cooking oil spray

- On a chopping board, cut through the layers of the lasagne pieces, separating each into three equal parts.
- Place a slice of cheese onto the bottom and middle pieces of lasagne. Then rebuild the lasagne: bottom piece, middle piece, then top piece. (*You will end up with the same two pieces of lasagne, except now they have slices of cheese inside.*)
- Grab three medium-sized bowls. Add flour to the first, beaten eggs to the second and breadcrumbs to the third. Dip the lasagne pieces into the flour and coat completely. Shake off any excess, then dip into the egg. Remove from the egg and dip into the breadcrumbs. Shake of any excess then dip back into the egg and then back into the breadcrumbs.
- Preheat air fryer to 180°C.
- Spray the base of the air fryer basket with cooking oil spray and place the pimped lasagne inside. Spray the lasagne with some more cooking oil spray.
- Cook at 180°C for 10 minutes, turning halfway, until breadcrumbs are golden brown and cheese is oozing.

INDEX

ACKNOWLEDGEMENTS

I **would not have been able to make this book without the** continual support of my family and friends. Mum, Dad, Joy, Kasey, Nate, Ant, Dennis, Brent, Shawn and my loyal offsider, Josh. A special mention goes out to my two doggos, Lexi and Rocco, for annoying me while I stumbled through the writing process.

A huge thank you to Emma and the Simon and Schuster team for believing in me. Rosie and Rosie for fixing my terrible punctuation and bad jokes. Brent and Meng for their amazing illustrations and design. Lawrence and Fiona for making my food look actually appetising.

Most of all I'd like to thank all of my followers on TikTok and Instagram. I don't know how we ended up here, but here we are.

I'd also like to say that it's good to remember that everyone is on a different path and everyone is different. So just do what you love, support others and everything will fall into place.

ABOUT THE AUTHOR

Jake Grigg is an Australian content creator and TikTok and Instagram sensation. Also known as the 'Air Fryer Guy', Jake boasts more than 1.5 million followers with over 10 million likes on TikTok alone. He is also an ARIA nominated singer and songwriter and writes jingles for all his air fryer videos.

Many households now have an air fryer in the kitchen and Jake has taken the idea of home cooking with an air fryer to new places by throwing any ingredient he can find into the air fryer and documenting what comes out. He believes that creativity is one of the most important parts of cooking, turning favourite naughty treats into air fried goodness. Each air fryer creation is mind blowing, eye catching, topical and DELICIOUS!